How to Become a Focus Ninja & Apply the Best Productivity Hacks Series

Simple Tips to Help Your Double Your Productivity, Achieve All Your Goals, Get More Done in Less Time, and Stop Procrastination

A.V. Mendez

2-Book Bundle Content:

HOW TO FOCUS

54 Habits, Tools and Ideas to Create Superhuman Focus, Eliminate Distractions, Stop Procrastination and Achieve More With Less Work

A.V. Mendez

TABLE OF CONTENTS

Introduction

Focus is a currency that is hard to get nowadays because we live in a world full of distractions.

So, what can we do about it?

How can we achieve maximum focus?

How can we make sure that we don't waste our time?

The answer is to build habits and follow ideas that help us eliminate distractions. The answer is to set ourselves up for success by changing our mindset and by building a tougher resistance to distractions. The answer is to combine different ideas for us to maximize our results.

Are you ready? Let's get started.

P.S. This book is *as straight to the point type of book as you can get.* I don't make it longer just to earn more money from Amazon. I make it as long and as short as necessary. My goal is not to give you hundreds of pages of useless information. My goal is to get you to take action one day at a time. I hope that the book's structure lends itself to doing just that.

HOW TO FOCUS

This book will give you 54 ideas that you can implement one by one so you can increase your ability to focus. Each idea includes an *Action Guide* that serves as the main lesson that you can apply to maximize the learnings and turn them into something concrete. You don't have to do all of them but I highly recommend that you try as much of the ideas as possible. They're all easy-to-implement mini-lessons that when added up, leads to a more focused way of life. Good luck and let's get this thing going!

1 - The Pomodoro Technique

The Pomodoro technique changed my life. Before *the Pomodoro,* I waste 30-45 minutes every day before I start working!

After implementing the Pomodoro, my habits changed and I was able to focus immediately on my work.

The Pomodoro forces my butt to take action.

The Pomodoro is basically about working in time chunks.

It's usually 25 minutes of work, then 5 minutes of rest.

Then you work again for 25 minutes and then rest for 10-15 minutes.

And then you just repeat the process over and over again until you finish your chosen task.

I use either tomatotimers.com (free) or a physical tomato timer.

I recommend that you focus on only one type of task per 1 Pomodoro cycle. This helps you focus your mind and not let it wander everywhere.

You can also use the method in any task that you want. You can use it for writing, managing your employees, meetings, chatting with customers, and even napping!

I also recommend that you use it on your hardest tasks. For example, if you're a content creator, then the hardest part of your task is creating content every day.

Go test the Pomodoro method and follow the 25/5/25/10-15 workflow.

There's a reason why every productivity coach out there teaches this method.

Simply put, **it works**.

Fun Fact: I almost didn't put this idea just because I know that every book out there about focus and productivity already discussed this method. But I realize that I will be doing a huge disservice for those people who may have never heard of it.

Go use it, it works!

Acton Guide:

Identify your most important task of the day and apply the Pomodoro Technique. Use www.tomatotimers.com (I'm not getting paid to promote this) or buy a physical timer on Amazon or your local shop.

2 - The "No Device" Principle

This one is hard to implement but is already something necessary to do.

Unless you really need a device in your desk to finish the work you are doing, I highly recommend that you put your mobile phones, iPads, and any other device in another room.

The harder for you to grab your device, the more unlikely it is for you to use it.

This will save you so much time and energy that you'll be able to finally focus more on the things that you want to do.

This is more of a habit than willpower.

Before you start your work, go ahead and put your devices on places that are hard to reach. If you're in the office, put your phone on your locker or below your desk.

Also, put them into silent mode as well.

Make this a habit and watch your focus increase by at least 2 folds! Guaranteed!

Action Guide:

What are the devices you have that only serves as a distraction every time you do your work?

Ask yourself, do you really need that device to achieve the goals you set for yourself that day? Or is it just something that you put beside you because it's a *habit*?

Most likely, it's just a bad habit that you developed over the years. Well, now it's time to let go of that destructive habit.

It's time to finally take control of your own agenda.

Identify these devices and then put them away.

You'll be doing yourself a big favor. Your productivity and ability to focus will increase, and you'll start to wonder how much time you could've saved if you only applied this technique years ago.

Don't be guilty though… Just apply what you learned and start today!

3 - Set a Daily Task

Even before the day starts, I always already know what things I should be working on for the day.

How?

The night before, I always create a list of *daily tasks* that I will do for the next day.

I start by making a list of the most important tasks that will have a big effect on my goal.

Next, I prioritize my task from *most important to less important.*

Then I make sure that I only have a maximum of 3 tasks per day. Too much on the list can demotivate us. Also, we tend to underestimate the time we need in order to finish a specific project. Limiting your tasks to 3 will give you more flexibility in finishing all your projects for the day.

Let's say that I'm an online guitar teacher.

My daily tasks could be the following:

1 - Creating guitar tutorials

2 - Editing the videos

3 - Posting videos on YouTube

4 - Creating online courses

5 - Marketing online courses

6 - Customer service

7 - Administrative tasks

8 - Financial planning for the business

9 - Advertising management

As you can see here, doing all of these in one day is impossible especially if you're a *one-man business*. So, you have to identify which tasks you should be doing every day.

Most likely, it'll be guitar tutorials and product marketing. So, start your day with the creation part and then use the other half of your day on marketing. Then on other days, you can focus on creating online courses content and managing your advertisements.

You don't have to do everything in one day.

Put your focus on 2 tasks and then add more if you still have lots of extra time.

Action Guide:

Make a list of the tasks that will have a huge effect on your goal. Out of all those tasks, what are the top 3 most important stuff? What are the *must-do*? What are the things that have a direct impact on your goals? Do them first and then add other other things if you still have time to spare.

4 - Meditation Works

A lot of people misunderstands this word. They think that meditation is only about being silent and doing nothing, trying to achieve *nirvana*.

We have too many thoughts and these things distract us every day. Meditation is about calming your mind.

It's been proven to lower our stress levels and helps us think clearly.

So how do you do meditation if you're easily distracted?

The answer is you start small.

Instead of going for 30 minutes of silence, you can start with 2 minutes.

Here's what I personally do:

I put in an earplug so I can have silence. Then I shut the lights off, set a 2-minute timer and then go to the corner of my room.

I breathe in for 3 seconds, and I breathe out for another 3. I listen to my breath. I don't try to not think about anything.

I just imagine my breath going from my nose to my tummy and then vice versa.

This simple way of meditation is what helped me fight that initial resistance to meditate.

After 1 week of doing this, I increased my meditation time to 5 minutes… and then ten…. I'm up to the point that I do it now in 15-20 minutes per day.

I don't know the exact science behind it. All I know is that it helped me focus more, sleep better and be less irritable.

I'm more patient now compared to before I started meditating. And as woo-woo as this sound, life is just more peaceful for me.

Maybe I did achieve nirvana. Maybe it's my own definition of nirvana. Peace, quiet, calm and patience.

Action Guide:

Start small if you must. If you have never tried meditation in your entire life, then start by doing it in your own chair. Do this now… Close your eyes, put your hands beside you, then breathe in and breathe out for 3 seconds each. Repeat the cycle 5 times and then open your eyes when you're done.

That's it. That's how you get started with meditation. No need to buy apps or any meditation devices for now.

Once you've done the exercise, increase your breathing cycle to 10.

Go make it a process. You don't have to do it all in one day.

5 - Use a Calendar App

Truth be told, I've never been a calendar app guy.

But when I went into sales, I realized how important they can be. Sure, not every job needs it, but if you can maximize its use, then it'll help you become more productive and it'll help you to be more focused on the right things.

So how do you use a calendar app?

To-Do List

You can put your to-do list on your calendar app. This helps you in streamlining the process. You can input one task and include the time frame needed for you to finish that certain task.

Appointment List

Another thing you can use it for is by setting appointments or meetings.

Since you can connect your Desktop app to your mobile app, you can easily look at your schedule and instantly know whether you have an appointment or not.

This also assures that you won't miss any meetings or client appointments just because you *forgot about it*. This is an unacceptable reason so make sure that this won't happen to you.

For Mac, I usually just use my stock Calendar app included in the laptop itself. You can also connect this to your iPhone's calendar app.

For PC users, I recommend that you use Google Calendar. You can then connect it to your Google Calendar App which you can download whether you're using iOS or Android.

Action Guide:

Choose a calendar app that works for you.

You can start with the basics:

For Mac and iOS (iPhone, iPad,) - Calendar App for Mac/ Calendar App for iOS

For PC/Other Laptops - Google Calendar for PC/Google Calendar for iOS or Android

Check out these links for some of the best apps that experts are using and recommending:

https://www.slant.co/topics/855/~best-calendar-apps-for-android

https://www.tomsguide.com/us/pictures-story/442-best-calendar-apps.html

Some of them are paid and some are free.

If you're only getting started, just start with free. Then upgrade as your needs increase.

6 - Teach People to Set an Appointment

Time Vampires.

That's what you get when people do not respect the value of your time. You have people texting, emailing, messaging, and going to your office door saying "let's talk, it'll only take a minute."

And of course, it's always never *just a minute.*

You see, these time vampires are everywhere! So, you have to guard your time like a Doberman guards its owner's house.

What I do is I teach people to set appointments.

If someone texts me, and it's not urgent, I always answer on a specific time frame (5pm-5:30pm). My phone is always on silent and has an automatic voice message that says I don't answer calls. I ask them to text me and I'll call them myself if it's an urgent matter. I make sure to stress that I don't reply to messages or calls because it affects my productivity.

It's the same with Facebook messenger. I only check it once every 2 days and honestly, I never had an urgent message on Facebook. It's always people asking for something. It's more of *can you do this for me? Can you send this? Here's a generic question, can you give an answer to this?* I just "seen" messages and don't reply unless I really needed to.

Another time vampire are meetings! OMG. Please, you don't need to run daily meetings! Unless you're in sales, then it's not needed.

What I do is I tell my staff that all our meetings will be done standing up. Guess what? Some kind of magic happened. Our meetings are all finished within 5-15 minutes. This saved me an extra 1-2 hours a day doing something more productive.

Action Guide:

Identify who are the time vampires in your life.

Where do they come from? *Facebook? Meetings? The "got a minute?" people in the office?*

Then teach them to set an appointment or to relay their message on hours that you're not busy working on your "must do" tasks.

This will save you so much time you'll wonder why you haven't implemented this before in your life.

7 - Time Chunking

Time chunking is scheduling your work hours in time chunks. So instead of working 2 hours straight, we can do something like this:

0:00 - 45:00 - Work
45:00 - 55:00 - Rest
55:00 - 1:30 - Work
1:30 - 1:40 - Rest
1:30 - 2:00 - Work

This helps you manage and maintain your energy. If you work on a very demanding job, then this will help you in keeping your productivity levels high throughout the day.

The difference between Pomodoro and Time-Chunking (TC) is that Pomodoro is just a Time Chunking Technique. TC is the foundation, Pomodoro is the implementation.

So how can you do TC the most effective way?

The key is to test what works for you.

For some, the Pomodoro time-frame works for them. 25 minutes of work, 5 minutes of rest, then repeat the process.

However, for people who lacked focus and attention, then you probably need more than 25 minutes (so you can sort yourself out first). I suggest starting with 50 minutes of work and then 10 minutes rest.

And yes, you do need to rest. In fact, it's the main secret why time-chunking works. Our body and brain needs the rest. There's just no way we can perform on a daily basis without taking a break. It's impossible to do it long-term.

Also, as your work day goes by, the more rest you need to schedule.

If you've already scheduled 5 cycles of *50 minutes of work and 10 minutes of rest* in the morning, then change it to *35 minutes of work, and 5-10 minutes of rest cycle* in the afternoon.

This will help you maintain your productivity level while still being effective at what you do. The goal is obviously not just being productive. It's also about producing the best outcome you can do.

Action Guide:

Use the time-chunking method on your next task. If you're easily distracted and needs time to adjust before working, then schedule a 50-minute time-chunk for work and 10 minutes for rest.

The first 10 minutes will be the hardest. It's the resistance phase of the game. You'll fumble, go to FB, Twitter, YouTube, and every other website just to avoid work. Give yourself permission to fail in your first few tries of the TC method.

Don't judge yourself too early in the game. Eventually, you'll learn to let go of the distractions and learn to just *do the work.*

8 - Use the Right Background Music

Listening to music has been proven to make us calmer and makes us more productive.

However, there is no one-size fits all type of music.

One type of music may calm you but the same music may make me anxious. The best that I can do is show you what works for me and some of my staff in the office.

Classical Music

For creative tasks, listening to Mozart and Beethoven works best. I don't know what's in their music, but it makes you think clearly and it helps in letting the ideas fly.

White Noise

We're creatures of nature. For millions of years, we evolved with lots of noises in the background. The trees, the birds, the animals, the breeze of the air, etc. So, it's no surprise to me that lots of people recommend working with white noise in the background as it makes them feel calmer and more "in tuned" with the nature.

Music Loop

For some, listening to the same music until it fades into the background becomes their shield against the world. The music loop becomes the background, and you start to put them on the side of your subconscious, allowing you to focus on the main task.

Favorite Spotify Playlists

I've asked a lot of people and random music from Spotify works best when they are doing administrative tasks. My theory is when you're listening to your favorite music, the admin tasks (which can be boring) becomes really exciting to do.

Action Guide:

I recommend starting with classical music. It's the safest choice and it's something that works for almost everyone. It doesn't matter what your job is. It's always a pleasure to listen to Mozart no matter what the situation is. Just don't use the same music when you're trying to get to sleep.

Check out this article to find the best classical music for focusing on your work.

https://www.independent.co.uk/student/student-life/Studies/classical-music-and-studying-the-top-10-pieces-to-listen-to-for-exam-success-a7037841.html

9 - Find "Your" Location

Your work location can also have a big impact on how focus you can be.

Some people swear that the natural noise from coffee shops works for them. Some people like to feel the vibe of having a co-working space. Then for some (like me), we prefer the space in the corner of the room.

Coffee Shop

If you'll work at a coffee shop, then expect it to be noisy. Expect that there will be more distractions. *That pretty girl in front of you drinking her chocolate frappe. That guy on his iPhone playing pubg. Or the sound of the coffee machine grinding all those gears to make you the best coffee possible.*

So, make sure that you're adept to working in this kind of environment.

Also, you can use coffee shops as your alternative office for doing administrative tasks. Think of it this way. The office is for production, and the coffee shops are for management.

Co-working Space

Another one that can get noisy at times is co-working spaces. If you work at home and you're already bored of always working alone, then you can feed with the energy of other people who's *just like you.* Lots of people in co-working spaces are startups or self-employed freelancers who can choose to work at home if they want to.

Office Space

If you're an employee, then you'll have fewer options where you can work. 90% of the time, you will be working in the company office. This is where time vampires hang-out a lot! So just be wary of who you talk to on a daily basis. Everyone's out there with their own agendas. Make sure that you're guarding yours like a kid guarding her candies.

Your Own Room

This works for me whenever I'm writing. I just can't do it in the office when there's a handful of people, who at any time can distract my workflow. I recommend this to anyone working on a creative task like writing, painting, coming up with ideas, and planning in general.

Action Guide:

Find a location that fits your task. Most creative endeavors require silence, while management stuff can still thrive in chaos.

10 - Create a To-Do List

To-do list has gotten a bad rap lately. I keep seeing lots of people on my Facebook feed saying that to-do lists are for average people. LOL.

The problem is not in the to-do list itself, it's in the way people create and implement their to-do lists.

If you're a lazy person and you have a list of 10 things to do per day, then your to-do list will not work!

I recommend no more than 7 of specific things to do every day.

Also, in case you're wondering, the difference between a to-do list and a daily task is that a to-do list is more specific.

A daily task may be this: write my book

A to-do list may look like this: write 1,000 words in 1 hour - (9am-10am)

It's more specific and it is time-bounded at the same time.

HOW TO CREATE A TO-DO LIST THAT WORKS.

1 - Start with the most important stuff. *If you're a real estate agent, then your most important task is to get clients.*

2 - Create a specific list of 3 things to do in the morning and 3-4 in the afternoon. The first 3 should be the most important and

urgent tasks. If you're just getting started with to-do lists, then only put 2 tasks in the morning and another 2 in the afternoon.

3 - Track your to-do list every day. *How many hours does it take to finish certain tasks?* You should know these things so you can create the correct time-frame for finishing them on your future to-do lists.

Action Guide:

Start creating a to-do list and only put a maximum of 4 things to do in the beginning. Too many tasks will make you feel overwhelmed, which may lead you to not take action in the first place.

Follow the 3-step process above to get started.

11 - The Lighting Matters

The room's lighting affects the ambiance of your workplace.

Too much light and it'll be almost distracting, too little and you'll start to feel like you're working with your eyes closed.

There are also some rooms with yellow lights in them (I hate those lights).

My recommendation is that you use a white Philips type of bulb. Bright enough that you can see what you're working on but not too much, that it's already affecting the reflection on your screen.

This is a simple tweak, but effective nonetheless in improving your focus.

Action Guide:

Check this website out to find the best type of light for you.

http://www.lighting.philips.com/main/prof/led-lamps-and-tubes/led-bulbs/sceneswitch-ledbulbs

Email their customer service if you have some important questions to ask.

12 - Stop Multitasking

It seems like there's a never-ending debate whether multitasking works or not.

Here's the truth. IT DOES WORK. But not in a positive way.

Sure, you can do 2 things at a time. But you'll never be as effective as you do when you focus on just 1 thing at a time.

This isn't even a debate anymore. Multitasking just plain sucks when it comes to maximizing our effectiveness.

We only think that it's working because we're finishing 2 tasks.

But the truth is, we can finish those 2 jobs faster and more effectively if we only do them one at a time.

The problem lies in our ability to re-focus.

When you do 2 things, your brain needs to adjust to the other task before it can completely recalibrate.

Don't believe me? Go do your main task for 20 minutes straight and then go watch YouTube for 10 minutes. I guarantee you that there's a good chance that you won't be as focused as you when you return to your original task. Your brain is in work mode and then you put entertainment time in there. The brain gets confused and now, it needs the time to re-adjust to your new mindset.

So, stop multitasking!
It works in making you feel like you're getting things done.

But it's an illusion. Focusing on one task at a time makes you more effective and efficient.

Multitasking makes your brain confused and it lets you wander off, thus making you waste precious time that you could've used on a more productive manner.

Action Guide:

Whenever you caught yourself multitasking, stop, close your eyes and breathe in and out 3 times. Then stop doing the other task or close the tabs that are not needed on your main task. Fight the urge to open social media sites or any blogging or news websites.

If you're writing, then write. Don't open YouTube and watch the highlights of your favorite team. Schedule that for later instead!

If you're calling prospects, then call and do nothing else! Don't start planning for lunch or stop cleaning your desk. Focus on understanding what your prospect is saying.

Stop multitasking. Stop multitasking. Stop multitasking.

I hope I'm clear about that. :P

13 - Do Your Most Important Task First

The reason why I stress doing the most important task first thing in the morning, is that I understand the way our mind and body works.

Mornings are when we have the most energy. Lunch and beyond is just a bonus in my book.

So how you identify your most important tasks?

First, you have to know your goal.

What do you want to achieve? If you're a songwriter, then the most important activity in your day will be songwriting.

In this case, you must spend the first 2-3 hours of your day writing songs.

Remember this. **Morning is for creating, and the afternoon is for marketing and management.** This applies to a lot of jobs out there.

Obviously, this may be different for some.

Let's say that your job is an English teacher. And let's say that your main task is *to teach Asian executives how to speak proper English.* If possible, try to schedule your sessions in the morning. Then use the afternoon for getting referrals and marketing your services. If you're just starting out and you don't have clients yet, then you can do this in vice versa. Focus on getting clients in the morning, then do your teaching sessions in the afternoon.

Action Guide:

Identify your most important task.

This is the task that will bring in the results that you want to get. What's important to you doesn't have to mean, that it's also the most important to someone with the same job that you have. Your goals and your progress in the field might be different, so your priorities will be different as well.

So, you can't just compare what you do to what others in your field does.

Find your own *"main task of the day"* and start doing them in the mornings.

14 - Visual Reminders

These are physical and digital reminders of things to be focusing on.

They don't have to be the tasks you should be doing (although you can certainly do that). You can add motivational quotes or pictures that inspire you to focus and go back to taking action.

They could be in the form of printed pictures, sticky notes, refrigerator magnets, and notes on your computer.

Action Guide:

Create your own visual reminders to maximize motivation and focus.

If you're having trouble remembering your daily tasks, then write it on a sticky note and post in your computer or your desk.

You can also put words of encouragement around you by posting printed motivational quotes.

These are just things that remind you to keep going.

This is a simple trick that gives me that extra boost to keep on working and to avoid my usual distractions.

15 - Build Your Willpower

Although it's never a good idea to only rely on your willpower, it does help to have some of it.

I think it's most important when you're just in the process of starting something.

You need that initial boost of willpower that will take you from procrastinating and being all over the place, to finally doing the task you're supposed to be doing.

So how do you build your willpower?

Well, you feed it.

You do it be fighting the resistance.

Let's say that your main task for the day is to call your prospects. Willpower thrives by feeding action into it.

What you can do is to start looking at the task as if it is a puzzle. You finish it piece by piece…

So, if you're calling a prospect to sell something, here's what it would look like:

First, you grab the phone… that's it. That's your first goal.

Now you have a piece of the puzzle and you just added a tiny amount of willpower in you.

Next, you hold the phone and put it in your ear. That's another step. Then you dial. Then you start talking... and so on.

This may seem like a ridiculous way to look at it, but the strategy just flat out works! They say that the pros don't need willpower to take action. They just need discipline to actually do the work.

But we're all not "pros" here... at least not yet.

So it's still nice to have some willpower that can take you over the hump of starting out.

Action Guide:

Start building your willpower by feeding it with small actions. This brings positive reinforcement and your brain starts to remember all these small wins and how it makes you feel. This adds to your willpower, thus making it stronger over time.

The more you feed it, the stronger it becomes.

The more you take action, the more your willpower becomes a strength of yours, ready to back you up and help you achieve maximum focus.

16 - Work Chunking (The Secret to Getting Started)

One of the hardest parts of getting things done is trying to start a project. The harder the task is, the harder it is to get started.

What we can do is apply the work-chunking method so we can fight the initial resistance of starting a project.

It's the same concept from the last idea I showed you. But this time, we'll take it to the next level by giving you more examples of how to do it.

Okay, say you're a copywriter and you were asked to create a sales page. The only problem is you're not in the mood to take action and you'd rather sleep all day... also, the deadline is in 3 days.

So how do you focus on your work and how do you even start?

This is where work-chunking comes in.

We can break-down the task that we're about to do, and implement small actions that lead to us finishing our task.

In our example, it's about creating a sales page.

A sales page has many parts but the basics are headlines, introduction, benefits via bullet form, product information, and call to action.

Instead of thinking "sales page" as a whole, we can trick our brain to focus on the headline first. Just say it "I'll **only** do the headline."

Then you start coming up with ideas for the headline. Next, you'll say "I'll only do the introduction"... then you come up with an introduction... then you just repeat the process over and over again.

It's about focusing on the steps within your chosen task, one idea at a time.

Action Guide:

Think about the tasks that you do on a daily basis. Ask how can you apply the work-chunking method on all of these tasks?

Break down the steps needed on every task, and set a time frame for finishing each step if possible.

Work-chunking is powerful; you just have to use it the right way.

17 - Batch Similar Tasks

One of the ways to avoid getting overwhelmed by things to do is to batch similar tasks. On our daily tasks, we tend to do 3-4 different categories depending on the job that you have.

These 4 categories are Creation, Management, Marketing, and Administrative.

Batching the tasks creates less confusion and it streamlines the process for getting things done.

I recommend that you do anything related to Creation in the morning. Tasks like creating content, writing, creating your product, etc.

After the creation part, you can either do the management or the marketing part. And the last category you can focus on is the administrative part of the business.

If you already have employees, then this can all be done simultaneously. However, I still recommend that you focus on the creation or production part first thing in the morning.

Action Guide:

Make a list of all the things that you or your business does on a daily basis. Just create a mindmap and dump all the information.

Next, create 4 columns on an excel file and categorize all the tasks via Creation, Management, Marketing or Administrative.

I guarantee you that you'll help streamline the process, and you'll gain more clarity in what tasks you or your business should really be doing every day.

18 - Set a Due Date/Deadline

All of the things I do related to my business has due dates or deadlines. Why? Simply because it's an effective way to save time and to make sure that we're actually getting things done.

If the tasks that you do doesn't have a deadline, then it's probably not important enough to do now!

The problem with some of the to-do lists that people create is they do not put a deadline so they end up not doing the to-do list in the first place.

I don't care of it's just a "quick task." Define what quick is because time is relative to the task. 30 minutes might be quick for some but someone else may see it as too slow.

So set deadlines and make sure that you're following a strict rule of finishing in those deadlines. If you found that your deadlines are too fast for you to handle, then simply change the deadline on your next (but the same type of) project.

Assessing Time-Frame

The bigger the goal, the further away the deadline will be. Some goals need 2 years and some needs 2 months.

Track your progress and evaluate if you're moving in the right direction. Remember, you can always pivot in the right way, but the first step in doing that is realizing that you are moving in the wrong direction. I can't stress this enough, always re-evaluate your situation and goals, and make sure that you're moving to and not further from the goal.

Action Guide:

Look at the main goals that you have. Assess the situation and be honest at what you'll find. Are you moving forward or backward? Pivot if you must. Then start setting hard deadlines.

These are not just *deadlines for show*. These are deadlines that you would actually want to beat. There will be long-term deadlines and there will be short ones. The way to beat the long-term ones is by making sure that your daily and weekly due dates are getting beat as well.

19 - Prepare Your Digital Workload

I always prepare all the tools that I need **the night before the workday.** I work on my computer so what I do is I open all the tabs that I need for my work and pin them through the Google Chrome Tab Pin function.

I also open all the folders, word file or any application that is needed for me to finish my most important tasks.

Anything that I don't need is strictly not to be opened.

I also hide all the files on my desktop for the time being, so I don't get distracted and open random stuff on my computer.

Doing this helps you set yourself up for success.

If all the tools that you need are already there, it is more likely for you to start taking action, instead of fumbling around wasting your time on nonsense stuff.

Action Guide:

Identify the tasks that you need to do tomorrow.

Next, identify the tools you need in order to finish those tasks.

30-60 minutes before you sleep, open your computer and open the tabs (pin them), applications and other digital tools that you need in order to successfully finish your *to-do* list.

20 - Declutter Your Digital Workload

Another way to help you focus on your tasks is to declutter your digital workload.

There are so many things that you can do that will help your ability to focus, these are the most important ones I personally did:

1 - Email subscription

I recommend unsubscribing to most of the emails you receive. Trust me, you don't need that coupon to buy a jerky beef, you don't need to follow 10 internet marketing gurus to learn Facebook ads, and you certainly don't need TMZ sending you "breaking news" about some idiot celebrity.

Add all these subscriptions up and you'll quickly realize how much time you're wasting on other people's agenda. These are digital time-vampires! Avoid them as much as you can.

2 - Desktop Apps

Another thing you can do is to delete some apps that you're not using anymore. They only serve as possible distractions for you. Plus, the constant *update this app* notification can also waste your energy you could've used on being productive.

Next, arrange your desktop apps by function. Put the word, excel and PowerPoint apps together. Then put all your editing apps together as well - stuff like photoshop, Camtasia, etc.

If they fit in one category, put them close to each other so you can easily find them when you're about to use them.

3 - Arrange Folders

This one is a biggie, and you probably need to take half a day to a whole day of free time to manage your folder and files.

What you can do is create a folder for videos, word files, images, and projects.

4 - Minimize Social Media Usage

Spending time on social media, especially if it's not work-related, is a waste of time. There's just no other way to describe it. It's a waste of time and it's stupid.

I recommend only using Facebook, Twitter, Instagram, and YouTube once every 2 days. Schedule your social media time if you have to. 20-30 minutes for each app is plenty.

Action Guide:

Schedule your "digital declutter work day" and choose one or two you can fix on that day. You can start with e-mail since it's the easiest thing to do. Check out this link to know more about finding and unsubscribing to most of your subscriptions.

https://www.pcworld.com/article/3181014/3-tools-for-easily-unsubscribing-to-emails.html

21 - Declutter Your Work Environment

Now it's time to focus on your physical environment. For years, I refused to clean my home-office on a daily basis. I reasoned that "I'm just a messy guy, that's who I am."

I didn't know at that time, but looking back, it's crazy how it affected my productivity. There's literally just stuff everywhere.

Papers, books, pens, water bottles, unwashed clothes, probably snakes (lol)...ugh, it's disgusting even to think about it now.

I didn't realize how it affected by mentality. Now, it's clear to me that having stuff everywhere really messes up with your flow. It's like there's distraction everywhere I look at.

But once I started to clean up my room (thanks Jordan Peterson), I became more productive, focused, less irritable and less prone to distractions.

It's honestly a whole new world for me! I'm not sure if you can relate, but maybe to a degree, you do.

I recommend that you declutter your work environment.

This will give you more focus and probably even less anxiety.

Start with the ones that you don't use. Throw them away or hide them on a room that you do not use.

Also, if you can't do it on your own, then hire a "Marie Kondo" type of professional who can help you manage your declutter.

Action Guide:

Schedule one-day off from work (or do it on weekends) and start decluttering your work environment.

If you work at home, then you probably need half a day to 3 days to finish it. However, if you work in an office, less than a day is more than enough.

Start with your desk. Throw away everything you do not need or give them away to an officemate.

Next, focus on paper works. Hide what you don't use anymore. 90% of the papers you have are probably useless now. Take the time to make sure that you actually don't need them anymore before you start shredding them.

22 - Use a Noise Cancelling Headphone

I work best when I'm at peace. I hate outside noise and I really can't stand being distracted.

I can be productive for 30 minute straight, and as soon as one guy comes over me and ask for something, I immediately turn into this unproductive mess of a person. For some reason, it'll take me up to 30 minutes again to gain back that lost focus.

So one day I decided to buy noise-canceling headphones.
It has two main benefits for me.

1 - I don't get to hear outside noises.

This is a big one for me. I'm easily distracted and I get irritable pretty fast. Not hearing other people's B.S. is worth its weight in gold for me.

2 - People stopped bothering me.

There's something about having a big headphone on your ear, people notice it and they're more likely not to bother you or talk to you. This saved me so much focus energy that I'd pay 10x the amount I paid for my noise-canceling headphone if I have to. It's just so worth it.

Alternatively, you can buy earplugs if you're working alone from home and you don't have as much distraction from other people.

Action Guide:

Go to your nearest store and look for a noise canceling headphone. It doesn't have to be ultra-expensive.

Also, you can search for best noise canceling headphones on Google and buy yours on Amazon.

I personally wouldn't pay more than $300 for one.

Here are some of the models you can look at:

1 - SONY WH-1000XM3 - $320
2 - BOWERS & WILKINS PX - $320
3 - BEATS STUDIO3 WIRELESS - $250
4 - SONY WH-1000XM2 - $350

Read the whole review here: https://www.t3.com/features/best-noise-cancelling-headphones

23 - Turn Your Notifications Off

You don't need the notification.

Repeat after me... "I DON'T NEED THE NOTIFICATION."

It'll only serve as distractions instead of reminders, and you know it too! So let's just go straight into taking care of this problem.

MAC

1.On your Mac, choose Apple menu > System Preferences, then click Notifications.
2.Select News in the list on the left, then set options on the right. To stop all notifications, click None. For more information about the options, click the Help button in the corner of the pane.

PC

1.On your computer, open Chrome.
2.At the top right, click More Settings.
3.At the bottom, click Advanced.
4.Under "Privacy and security," click Content settings.
5.Click Notifications.
6.Choose to block or allow notifications: Block all: Turn off Ask before sending.

iOS

1.Launch the Settings app on your iPhone or iPad.
2.Tap Notifications.
3.Select the app for which you want to turn on or off banners.

4.Toggle the Allow Notifications switch on if it's not already.

5.Tap Banners to enable or disable them.

Android

1.Go to Settings > Sound and Notification > App Notifications.

2.Tap the app you want to stop.

3.Tap the toggle for Block, which will never show notifications from this app.

Action Guide:

Choose the device that you have and follow the instructions above. I got them directly from their respective authority websites so it should work.

Remember, you can choose to turn on a specific app if you really need a notification for that application.

24 - Get Help

Not all of the tasks that we'll put on our to-do list are possible to be finished by us alone.

Sometimes, you just have to ask for help. Not all problems can be solved by focus alone. There will be tasks that require a combination of 3 people working together.

When focus is not enough, then you probably need another hand to work on the project.

There's nothing wrong with asking for help.

The sooner you discover you need help; the sooner you try to find someone who can help you.

Action Guide:

Look at the projects that you are doing alone. Does it feel like it's getting next to impossible to finish them?

Then you probably need to ask for help.

Ask an employee for support or hire a freelancer to help you finish some aspects of the project.

Ask for help, then refocus on parts of the job you assigned to yourself.

25 - Drink a Green Juice First Thing in the Morning

What you put in your body has a big effect on how you think. On one hand, eat junk food first thing in the morning and you'll feel bloated and groggy all day. On the other hand, drink green juice in the morning and you'll feel energized instead.

There's obviously lots of recipes out there. You can even create your own if you want too.

However, most of these green juice (created or packaged) taste bad... Some are even AWFUL. "Yuck" as my younger brother used to say.

What I do is I drink a green powdered juice that I can easily prepare.

Out of all the brands that I've tried, I only found one that doesn't taste like crap.

The brand is called Organifi Juice.

Their website is:

https://www.organifishop.com/

Look, I know that I'm biased, but I suggest that you try making your own green juice first and then buy Organifi and compare it.

Trust me, it won't be as good when it comes to the taste (Organifi taste like candy). Plus, you don't have to spend time in preparation and cleaning your juicing machine.

Action Guide:

Drink your green juice first thing in the morning. You'll immediately see an increase in your focus and energy levels within 7-10 days of consistently drinking it every day.

26 - Should You Avoid Caffeine?

If you've been consuming strong caffeine (coffee, tea, anything with caffeine) every morning, then it would be hard for you to not drink one before every work day.

I understand your dilemma. I've been a coffee addict for years, and it took me a few months to even minimize it since the day I decided to stop drinking coffee.

The thing about caffeine is you can get dependent on it. It would feel like you absolutely need it (which you don't). That's why I recommend green juice in the last chapter, so you can stop being dependent on caffeine for your energy.

Caffeine also gives you that crash after the initial boost of energy. I'm usually super energized for 2-3 hours and BAM! I'm done, I can't focus, and I can't work properly anymore.

What You Can Do

Here are some of the things you can do to minimize and then eliminate your dependency on caffeine.

1 - Replace it with a better alternative (Water or Green Juice)

2 - Drink less by having smaller servings. If you drink 1 full cup of coffee, then serve a ¾ cup instead… then you change it to ½ after a few weeks… reduce it bit by bit until you kicked off the habit.

3 - Don't blame yourself for wanting to have some of it. For me, I don't mind having coffee at least twice a week. I don't really crave for it anymore since I started drinking water + green juice every morning.

4 - Go from strong to mild. Change the brand of the coffee you're drinking. Look at the caffeine level that you're consuming and change it from strong to mild.

5 - Do not go to the coffee aisle when you are grocery shopping. You cannot consume it if you don't buy it in the first place.

Action Guide:

Choose one idea (from the suggestions above) that you can apply today.

You can either start small or you can go "all in" if you have the willpower to stop consuming caffeine.

27 - Preserve Your Emotional Energy

We only have a limited amount of energy that we can spend all day. This includes our emotional energy.

Emotional energy is defined by our psychological capacity to express and manage our emotion.

We don't usually notice it but a lot of us are emotionally spent.

Do you feel like you don't want to talk to anyone anymore after an 8- hour work day? Do you wish Sally from the accounting department would just *shut up for a minute*? Do you feel like you're going to snap at any time?

If yes, then you are emotionally spent.

Your emotional energy is already drained.

That's why you need to recharge it... but how?

First of all, avoid time vampires. Time vampires' super-power is to siphon energy without you even noticing it. You'll just walk out of the conversation feeling like your battery just got drained.

Second, manage your emotions during high-stress work days. Do not get too attached to everything that's going right or wrong. Law of Murphy says that "whatever can go wrong, will go wrong." Remember that you do not have any control to everything that's going to happen. Stop stressing about it and think about the solution instead.

Third, physical work out every morning (if possible) is proven to lower stress, which helps you recharge your emotional battery and helps you gain more focus. If you can't do it in the morning, try to do it in the middle of the day. Just sneak in a 30-minute session in there... Your last option is to do it at night, 2 hours before you sleep.

Action Guide:

Identify the things that are siphoning your emotional energy. Ask yourself, are you managing your emotions well when it comes to those things? How do you react whenever someone fails at the task that you gave them? Do you feel anxious, annoyed, and pissed off? Or do you feel calm, logical and reasonable?

Remember, focus on things that you can control. And most of the time, the only thing you have control over is the way you respond to certain situations.

28 - Say No and Mean It

Whenever we're dealing with time vampires, we tend to be too polite and say yes to their requests.

It's not that you want to say yes all the time. In fact, you know that you should say "no." But why do we keep saying yes when what we really mean is "no, I don't want to do it" or "no, I'm quite busy right now."

It's because we're afraid of conflict. We don't want people to feel bad or say bad things about us. So we become a "yes man or yes woman" and we gladly (or it appears on the outside) say yes to people's demand for our time and energy.

But this is a problem… and a big problem at that.

These distractions kill our focus and momentum. These distractions don't allow us to be the best version of ourselves.

So, you have to learn to say no…. And mean it!

Action Guide:

1 - Practice saying NO in the mirror. Seriously, just go in front of your mirror and say "NO" 30x-50x. Be comfortable in saying it. You're going to have to say no to a lot of things so you can say yes to the right things.

2 - Give "no" as an answer but give alternatives.

For example, someone wants "a minute of your time" but you really don't want them to always bother you this way.

What you can do is say no, and then explain why you're saying no.

It can go something like this:

"Hey Rob, I understand that you need help right now, but I'm going to have to say no. I'm very productive during 8-11am and I want to keep my momentum going forward. When it comes to these requests, I would really appreciate if you could ask them at least a day before the meeting or during the afternoon. Thanks, buddy."

It will seem weird or awkward at first to have to explain yourself, but you only have to do it once or twice. Once they are trained to accept your response, you'll now have less distraction and you just turned that time vampire into a productive friend.

29 - Say Yes, But Only If It Matches Your Goals

Now, you don't have to say no all the time as well!

You also have to say yes to new opportunities…. But only if it matches your goal.

Let's say that Sonny, VP of your company, wants you to meet a person coming over dinner at 7pm. If that guy can help you in your goals, then you should be open in canceling your original plan for the night. You should weigh the pros and cons of attending that dinner. You should know the consequences of your decisions.

So, say yes to opportunities, not all people who approach you are time vampires. Some will have the ability to help you in achieving your goals.

Action Guide:

What opportunity has shown up in your life recently? Make sure that you weigh the options of saying yes or no.

Is it really worth it missing your kid's soccer game while you attend an all-day meeting? Sometimes it's worth it and sometimes, it's not.

Learn to evaluate the situation and make a decision that you would stand for. Another thing to look at is the opportunity cost. You saying yes to one thing means you're saying no to another. Again, weigh your options. Choose the one that is more important to you, and stand by the decision you make.

30 - Exercise Every day

This is common knowledge. Exercise helps you become physically healthy, more energized, be happier, gain more focus, etc.

The problem is not about knowing how to exercise. The problem we have is in the discipline of implementation.

Most of us feel like we don't have the time to exercise.

With kids, our work, vacations, etc., there's just no way we can do it anymore, right?

But lots of people who are busy still manage to exercise every day or two. The key is to make it a part of your day. It's something you do like brushing your teeth or taking a shower.

What I suggest that you do is to start with a 15-minute workout routine. Most of us will have 15 minutes to spare, and it wouldn't really take too much out on our schedule.

There's a lot of 15-minute workouts that you can follow... seriously, just Google "15-minute workouts" and you'll find hundreds to choose from.

For your convenience, I put a sample 15-minute workout below that you can follow.

Action Guide:

Check out this link and follow the instructions. Working out, even for just 15 minutes will have a positive impact on your energy levels and your ability to focus.

Apply the strategy mentioned below:

https://www.self.com/story/a-15-minute-no-equipment-workout-thatll-sculpt-your-abs-and-arms

The 15-Minute No-Equipment Workout

- Plank to Dolphin
- Push-up
- Plank Tap
- Forearm Side Plank With Twist
- Bicycle Crunch
- Plank to Downward Dog
- Diamond Push-up
- Lateral Plank Walk
- Boat Pose

31 - Take Short Walks

Here's a list of famous people who took short walks every day...

- Aristotle. ...
- William Wordsworth. ...
- Charles Dickens. ...
- Henry David Thoreau. ...
- John Muir. ...
- Patrick Leigh Fermor. ...
- Soren Kierkegaard.

And there's a reason why they did it...

Walking outside helps you regain clarity. It helps in relaxing our minds and letting it wander for a bit.

Miraculously, lots of new ideas may come up during or after a walk. It's as if the walking part gives birth to new ideas hiding in the back of our minds.

Honestly, I don't even try to know the reason why that happens... I couldn't care less.

All I know is that when I take short walks (10-20 minutes) outside, I always come back refreshed and full of new ideas brewing in my mind.

Action Guide:

Walk outside your house or office after 2-3 hours of focused work. 10-15 minutes outside will help your mind to relax and be ready for the next task ahead.

32 - Run, Run, Run

When it comes to the physical benefits, running has the same effect as walking.

In addition to the physical benefits, it also helps you regain clarity and focus for the work ahead of you. But unlike walking, it's best to do running on a longer time frame to maximize its benefits.

Walking is best for gaining clarity, while running is for building energy and endurance.

When it comes to running, I recommend that you do it 3x-4x a week at 1 hour each session.

Also, run outside if you can. Running on treadmills is ok, but not as beneficial as having the full experience of seeing nature and feeling the different sensations of the outside world.

Action Guide:

1 - Go get your own running shoes from any of the famous brands. However, do not spend more than $120 for a pair.

https://www.esquire.com/uk/style/shoes/g24739613/best-mens-running-shoes/

2 - Get yourself a wireless earbud. It's best to have one that is specifically made for running. Listen to motivational speeches, lessons about a topic you're interested in or listen to your favorite music to make running more fun

https://www.cnet.com/topics/headphones/best-headphones/best-truly-wireless-headphones/

3 - Plan your route. There are free and paid *running apps* out there that you can use every session. Don't go crazy on the details, start with the free one if you're at the phase of just trying to build the running habit.

https://www.telegraph.co.uk/technology/mobile-app-reviews/10237554/top-10-running-apps.html

33 - Sleep Soundly

(Disclaimer, I am not a doctor and all I'm going to suggest in this chapter is based on my own experience. Consult your doctor before you do anything that I suggest here).

With that said, I'm passionate about sleep.

Why? Because I know its importance in my life.

My worst days has always been the ones when I didn't get enough sleep. Whenever I sleep less than 6 hours, the next day doesn't seem to blend well for me.

I just cannot function properly without 7-8 hours of sleep.

It's been rumored that Einstein slept for 10-12 hours a day.

We're no Einstein so 7-8 hours is enough for us.

I've tried many sleep optimizations over the years, some of them are useless and a waste of money and some worked well for me.

Action Guide:

Here are the strategies that worked like a charm for me:

1 - Total Darkness

I made my room super dark that almost no outside light goes through inside. This helps me tremendously in getting asleep fast.

2 - 5-HTP

I've tried many sleeping aids and this has the best effect for me. It also helps that it doesn't give me any migraine, morning grogginess or any side effects the morning after.

3 - No Device 2 Hours Before Sleeping

All the devices that we use nowadays emits light that signals the eyes that "it's still morning," that's why it's hard to sleep when you're still on your phone at night. Our brains get tricked by this harmful blue light, thus making it hard for us to get to sleep. This also affects our sleep as we don't get to have a deeper type of sleep whenever we use our devices too much.

4 - Earplugs

Outside noises may wake us up in the middle of our sleep. I found that a small earplug helps eliminate some of the outside noise I may hear while I'm asleep.

Choose a smaller cut because putting earplugs 8 hours every night may start to physically hurt your ears.

34 - Take Short Breaks

We are in a culture of Hustle.

When the celebrity entrepreneur, Gary Vaynerchuk said that we should hustle, I think a lot of people misunderstood what he meant.

When he said "hustle," he didn't mean that we should work 18 hours a day and sleep 4 hours at night. It's not about how many hours of sleep you have. It's about what you're doing during your waking hours.

The truth is, not all of us has the ability to work more than 12 hours a day. It's physically and mentally tiring to do on a daily basis… almost impossible for some.

What we can do is to maximize our time instead. Make ourselves more focused and more productive. Part of that is taking short breaks…

All the strategies I mentioned before has *taking a break* included in them. Why? Because it's as important as the work itself. So, don't be ashamed of taking a break from the *hustle*. We need it for us to stay effective and efficient. We need it so we can continue being at our best.

Action Guide:

Go back to all the strategies I mentioned before (time chunking, work chunking, Pomodoro, etc.). Are you implementing the "break" part or are you ignoring them?

35 - Start and Follow a Morning Routine

We are a creature of habits and routine. Not having our routines affects our circadian rhythms needed for us to stay healthy - emotionally, mentally and physically speaking.

If you're a writer, the most effective way to build a writing habit is to write at the same time every day...

If you're a basketball player, having a regular sleep schedule can help you maximize your talents...

Whatever your work is, you can maximize your effectiveness by having some kind of routine that you do every day.

I recommend that you start with a morning routine.

These are things that you do in the first 1-2 hours of your day. This morning routine helps you set your day up for success.

Most successful people have their own versions of morning routines. A combination of; drinking water or something healthy, journaling, meditation, exercise, and writing are the usual tasks.

If you want to learn more about morning routines, I recommend the book Miracle Morning by Hal Elrod.

Action Guide:

1 - Create your own morning routine. It could be 15 minutes, 30 minutes or pretty much whatever you want. The goal is to do something that will set the mood and energy for the rest of the day. If you start your day with something productive, you are more likely to keep the spirit of productivity and get more things done for the day.

2 - Research more about things that you can do on your morning routines. Not all of the things that we'll try will work for us. So, research more and find more things you can try.

36 - Take Naps

So, you've done most of the ideas in this book and you've become very productive. You're maximizing your time and you're very focused in your work. But there's just one big problem.

By the time the clock hits 12 at noon, you already feel tired and spent. You spent so much energy in the morning doing your important tasks, and you don't feel like working anymore.

You're just too tired already. So, what's the solution?

Simple: Take a 10 or 20-minute nap.

Taking a nap is proven to help you gain alertness and focus the easy way. Just rest your mind and body for a little bit, and you'll instantly get that power boost that you need so you can work from 1pm onwards.

Action Guide:

1 - Schedule your nap time during lunch. Make sure that you follow the same schedule every day, and nap at the same exact location as well.

2 - Expect the first week to be hard. You won't easily be able to fall asleep. I suggest that you set the timer for 25 minutes on your first week since the first 10-15 minutes will most likely be the time you spend trying to fall asleep. Then go back to the 10-20 minutes' timer as originally planned.

3 - Set a timer for 10-20 minutes. Sleeping more than 20 minutes can have a negative effect on you. You'll feel groggy and you won't be able to focus on your work anymore. So, trust me, stick with a 10-20 minutes' nap.

4 - Use an earplug so you don't have to hear other people's B.S. during lunch. I'm serious, there's way too much gossip going on during break time. Make sure you don't hear any of that.

37 - Stretch Yourself - Part 1

Go do a stretching exercise after every 30 minutes of work. Our body isn't made to sit all day. We're made to hunt and move. But there's obviously no need for that now.

So, we have to move our body constantly in order to stay in shape. One of the best ways to battle back pain and body aches is to do stretching exercises.

A 1-minute stretching session is all that you need for every 30 minutes of work.

It's crazy how a 1-minute stretching session can relieve you lots of stress in your body. Try it, it works!

Action Guide:

Find a place where you can do your stretching exercise. If you can't, there are many stretching exercises that you can still do at your desk.

If you're following the Pomodoro, then use a part of the rest time for stretching. Do this consistently throughout the day in order to build the habit.

Resources

Check out these simple stretching exercises you can do.

For people who have extra space:

https://www.shape.com/fitness/workouts/only-5-stretches-you-need

Stretching exercise in the office:

https://www.themuse.com/advice/17-desk-stretches-thatll-almost-replace-going-to-the-gym

38 - Stretch Yourself - Part 2

The last idea was about stretching yourself physically.

For this one, I'm talking about stretching yourself mentally. It's about stretching your capacity to think. To know that "you can do better" and to know that you have so much more potential in you.

Often, when we start something hard, we start to realize that we are capable of so much more. My friend always says "Big problems, big money," His point isn't just about the money. It's about expanding ourselves for what we can truly do. It's about evolving and being better than we were before.

So, this is my challenge to you.

CHOOSE TO STRETCH YOUR CAPABILITIES.

Are you thinking too small? Are you underestimating your capacity? This not only applies in your ability to focus but also in other aspects of your self-improvement journey.

Action Guide:

Do you really lack focus or you're just afraid of doing the work? Each of us has the ability to expand. Choose to improve every single day and learn to stretch your thinking cap.

Ask yourself, in what area of your life are you thinking too small?

39 - Note Taking Apps?

I've always been wary of using note taking apps.

I still use pencils and notebooks for most of my notes, so I'm kind of old school in that way. So, do you really need all these note taking apps? The answer is it depends.

If you're in a business that requires you to organize lots of information, then these apps may help you streamline the process.

However, if you have a simple business or a job that already has a system in place, then just use what you already have in the workplace.

Note: *Maybe a simple "Notes" app from Mac or PC's version of it will do*

You can also choose to use the free versions of different note taking apps so you can decide whether you need it or not.

Action Guide:

Read this review and choose the right one for you.

https://www.lifewire.com/best-note-taking-apps-4136590

Also, ask yourself if you really need a note taking app.

Do you take that many notes every day to actually need it?

Or a simple pen and paper will do?

40 - Review Your Day

In order to continue being productive, you have to make sure that your daily tasks are being done properly.

More than half of your task list will probably be the same on a daily basis. That means you can evaluate your daily tasks and find a way to optimize your time.

How can you make this task simpler? How can you maximize your working hours while doing these repetitive tasks?

Action Guide:

Take note of the time frame needed to finish certain tasks and find a way to finish them faster.

So how do you do that?

First, you have to look at the hours you need to finish them.

Second, identify the actions that needs to be done.

And third, find a way to get things done fast - by either working faster and coming up with solutions faster or by outsourcing the task itself.

41 - Review Your Week

During Saturdays or Sundays, I always do a recap of the work-week that I had.

Did I achieve my daily goals? How many tasks did I fail to do? How many pending tasks do I have to finish for the next work week?

Asking these questions, and taking notes, allows me to track my progress every week.

This helps me have a bigger picture of where I'm at in my journey.

Am I moving too slow? Am I inching closer to my goal?

I will not know the answer unless I'm tracking my weekly progress.

Action Guide:

Do a weekly review of your progress...

First, see if you're finishing the majority of your tasks on a daily basis.

Second, are you finishing the tasks that are actually getting you closer to your goals? Just because you're taking action doesn't mean you're getting closer to your main goals. You can't just *do the stuff*, you also have to *do the RIGHT stuff*

42 - Review Your Month and Year

Up next is your monthly and yearly reviews.

This is where you make a deeper evaluation of your goals.

You may be focus and productive, and you're getting things done… but you still have to see if you're moving towards your goals.

Your monthly and yearly reviews should focus on your results.

Are you getting sales? Are you making a profit?

This also applies to any endeavor. If you're in boxing, you could see if you improved your quickness. In songwriting, you can look at how many songs you've written. These aren't things that you can evaluate daily or weekly. These are the things that takes some time.

Action Guide:

Look at the bigger picture and see if you're taking the right steps toward your goals. If your goal is to make 100k per year and you only made 20k by July, then you're obviously off the tracks. It's time to evaluate your actions. It's time to evaluate what you're doing and achieving on a monthly basis because something is clearly not working. Identify the problem, then create a better solution so you can achieve your goal.

43 - Do Not Be a Perfectionist

I got lucky I guess. Early in my career, I decided that I'd rather have *speed of implementation* rather than *perfectionism*.

Being a perfectionist can be dangerous because nothing is inherently perfect. There will always be something better. There will always be an improvement to make.

In fact, Apple's billion-dollar strategy hinges on this exact type of thinking - that "nothing is perfect, **but we can still improve.**"

Look at all their products, they're pretty and simple to use. Lots of people buy them. Are they perfect? No. Are they the most feature packed? No.

What they do is they make upgrades every year and they don't focus on making the products perfect. Don't get me wrong, they are good products - but perfect? No.

As long as they keep improving every year, then Apple will continue to exist.

The Dangers of Perfectionism

1 - You Don't Get Things Done

Instead of moving to the next project, the perfectionist wastes his time away trying to make something perfect. Instead of testing the market's response, the perfectionist spends 5 years on a product that no one asked for!

Getting things done (as long as they are good) is better than getting things perfect.

2 - You Waste Something Good

In our quest to perfectionism, we tend to throw away "the good stuff" that we already made. *You spent so much time and energy on that thing and you're just going to scrap it?* No, you wouldn't.

Why don't you ask for other people's feedback first? Just because you don't think it's perfect doesn't mean no one will ever like it.

3 - You Become Delusional

To a perfectionist, nothing is ever good enough. People will try their damn hardest and a perfectionist will still see garbage.

You not only demean other people by doing this... You also make yourself paranoid. You start aiming for unwarranted requests and bad expectations.

"But Steve Jobs was a perfectionist" Yeah, and his employees hated him for this. Steve Jobs wasn't fun to be around with, he was not a person you would like to eat your dinner with. Also, Steve Jobs actually learned to lessen his perfectionism, this allowed Apple to tap into more mass-market (but still premium) products - which made apple grew.

Stop being a damn perfectionist. Unless it's life and death we're talking about, sometimes, good enough is good enough.

Action Guide:

Read this article about Steve Jobs.

https://www.inc.com/jeff-haden/chasing-steve-jobs-why-perfectionism-is-your-worst-enemy.html

Decide for yourself that you would focus on SPEED OF IMPLEMENTATION instead of perfectionism.

Just to be clear, I'm not saying that you should do crappy work.

No, you should always strive to produce a product or a service that **your intended audience will like.**

The keyword here is INTENDED AUDIENCE.

Someone who likes to read complicated books won't probably like my book. They'll complain about my grammar and my sentence structure. They will hate that I write as if I'm just talking to a friend. But he's not my intended audience so I couldn't care less. I would rather give awesome and actionable content that will change other people's lives than to spend thousands of hours making my writing sounds like somebody who I am not.

44 - Schedule Your "Pleasure Time"

I already touched on this a little bit on the other chapters, but this is important so I want to talk about it more.

Your pleasure time is important. It's something that you need mentally and physically. We all need a break from work and it's something that we should schedule as well.

Here are the possible things you can do during your break time.

YouTube, Facebook, Twitter, and Instagram

Social media is something that you and most people spend time on every day.

So, schedule your social media time. For example, you can use 7-8pm as your "social media time." You can also put a little bit of "Insta Time" during your working hours.

8am-10:30am can be work and then use 10:30-10:45 as your Insta time.

The point is to not use social media randomly. Make your social media time deliberate. Schedule it as if it's part of the work. I found this to be an effective way **to stop** checking my phone randomly throughout the day.

Other Habits (Entertainment, Sports, TV, Video Games)

These are mostly done during the weekends. Stuff like watching a series, a sports game, or any kind of fun activity.

Make sure that you schedule them on the weekends

Use this as an opportunity to recharge and forget about your work. When you're doing these activities, focus solely on the fun stuff you are doing... Turn off the notification and **stop checking your phone** every 10 minutes. Just focus on having fun so you can make these activities worth doing.

Action Guide:

Schedule your "Pleasure Time." Make them part of your weekly schedule and things to do.

By doing this, you'll enjoy your break time more, and you are more likely to be focused when you start working on your tasks.

45 - Learn to Disconnect

Our electronic devices have become an extension of our lives that it's almost impossible to not use them. But having that one day of break is a good reminder about what really matters in our lives.

Once a month (usually by the end of the month), I go to someplace close to nature and I disconnect from my normal world.

I don't bring the mac or the iPad. I still bring my phone but I put it on silent (and will only check it the next day).

I just disconnect from everything and everyone I'm familiar with. I go to some place where nobody knows me.

Normally, I just go for a swim, a meditation session, a massage, or I write (on a notebook) about ideas I want to implement in the near future.

This allowed me to renew my energy and enthusiasm for my work.

I recommend that you do the same and see if it'll have the same effect for you.

Action Guide:

Go find someplace near you where you can do the Disconnect Day. Do not bring any devices unless you really need to. Just do random stuff that you don't normally do. DOING NOTHING is perfectly fine! If that relaxes your mind, then, by all means, do nothing!

Other activities you can do are:

1 - Learning to draw

2 - Calligraphy

3 - Surfing

4 - Swimming

5 - Biking

6 - Rock climbing

7 - Trekking

8 - Going to a museum

9 - Spending the day on a library

10 - Going to a zoo

46 - Avoid Your Email

The majority of us open our email first thing in the morning. This is a problem because we're opening ourselves up to early distractions. An email is basically just a list of other people's agenda. If you get 20 emails a day, and you spend an average of 3 minutes per email, then you'll be spending an hour a day dealing with other people's agenda.

That's not very productive to do, especially in the morning. So, if it's possible, and your work allows you to do it, avoid email as much as you can especially in the morning.
I only check my email twice a day.
Once at around 11am, and then once at 4pm.

Having the discipline to follow this routine will free up not only your time but also your mental load. Not having to think about too much stuff lets you focus on the task ahead.

Avoid your email and train people to notice your time frame. Better yet, let them know that you only check your email twice a day. Remember, **an email is just a list of other people's agenda.** Most emails don't need to have a reply. Choose the most important ones and stick to your schedule.

Action Guide:

Unsubscribe to the majority of your email subscriptions, except the necessary ones. Schedule your email time. Twice a day is plenty.

47 - Ask What the Process Requires

We get easily distracted when we don't know the next step in our task.

Let's say that you're a songwriter. When you run out of lyrics you can think of, then you suddenly open yourself up for distractions.

Not being prepared for this scenario can kill your focus and productivity.

So, you have to ask yourself what the process requires.

What can you do when these "lag" happens? What can you do to make sure that you'll get back to work?

Let me give you another example.

Let's say that you're a Virtual Assistant for Real Estate Ads on Facebook. If your company is good, then you would have a list of script to use for every answer the customer may say.

Knowing these scripts is part of the process. In fact, it is the process. Knowing these answers is what the process requires. So, you have to find a way to collect all the possible response from your customers and create a list of answers that you would say.

Whether you're in songwriting or Real Estate Facebook Ads, the point is to be ready in finding out a way to make the process seamless. The faster you find a solution, the less you are likely to give-in to distractions.

Action Guide:

Identify your most important tasks.

Ask yourself. "What are the aspects of these tasks that are more likely to have problems?"

Find those holes early in the process and find the best solutions you can think of.

This is not to say that you should look for problems that don't exist. No. This is about looking at the potential flaws of your project and being ready for what may happen because of those flaws.

48 - Work with Two Computer Monitors

If you've never had a 2-monitor setup before, then I guarantee you that you'll sing praise and hallelujah after you tried doing it.

Having that extra space of real estate allows you to open more tabs at the same time. This saves you time and energy in opening and closing tabs that you may use.

Having 2 monitors also allows you to view documents side by side. You can open one application for production and another one for research.

If you're a Facebook Ad Manager, you can open one side for the Facebook Ad itself, and then the other screen for your Facebook Page.

If you're a novelist, you can open one for Scrivener writing app, then the research materials for the other screen.

The possibilities are endless.

Don't worry if you're not super techie. There are lots of guides out there that you can use.

Just Google your computer model's name and add the word "dual monitor setup."

Action Guide:

Check out this article and find out what setup works for you.

https://www.lifewire.com/boost-productivity-with-a-second-monitor-2377817

https://www.pcworld.com/article/2057936/how-to-set-up-two-monitors.html

You don't have to be fancy with this. If all you can afford is the cheapest setup, then just go for it for now. Once you can already afford the more expensive ones, then go and upgrade to better monitors.

49 - Mindmap Your Ideas

Our brain has a hard time trying to make sense of all of our ideas at the same time.

So, whenever you have an idea for a project, I recommend that you create a brain dump via a mindmap.

This allows you to put your idea into writing.

If you're coming up with a business plan, then create a mind map and just scatter all your ideas into one main theme.

It could potentially look like this:

Source: https://www.kub-uk.net/business-ideas-generate-sales/

The point here is to just do a brain dump and write whatever comes to your mind. Our goal is to get the idea out of your mind and into the screen.

This gives us a better understanding of what we can do next.

This also helps us in focusing on the right idea. *Does this idea have its own legs? Does it look like you have enough knowledge or experience to actually implement this idea?*

The mindmap gives us a better idea of what we know and what we don't know.

Action Guide:

Create a mindmap whenever an idea comes up. You always want to put the ideas into writing, and the best way to do that is to create a brain dump.

Do not judge your idea too quickly. Let it brew and take your time in assessing whether it's worth implementing or not.

I personally use MINDJET because I found the UI to be clean and easy in the eyes.

Check out your other options here:

https://www.slant.co/topics/1798/~best-mind-mapping-tools

50 - Increase Your Attention Span

Increasing your attention span can be a big factor on whether you'll be able to focus or not.

The good news is your attention span is elastic like a rubber. You can train yourself to focus more, to keep your attention on a specific thing or task.

But your attention span won't increase in itself, you have to take the time to actually work on it.

Action Guide:

Here are the things you can do to increase your attention span:

Keep It Quiet

Too much noise can distract us and put our attention on other things. Keep it quiet and work in a room where noise cannot get in.

I already suggested that you buy an earplug or a noise canceling headphone. I want to repeat it here because based on my experience, they are the most valuable purchase I had, related to increasing my focus and productivity.

Memorize Stuff

Practice memorizing cards so you can expand your mental alertness. Buy a set of playing card and practice memorizing by starting with 10 cards.

Shuffle them and then look at it for a few seconds, then practice memorizing the order of the cards.

Stay Hydrated

A study at the University of Barcelona that a 2% decrease of water in our body has a huge effect on our mood and ability to focus. Always have water beside you and drink every 30 minutes or so.

51 - The Do Not Disturb Sign

It's crazy how effective this can be.

When you have a sign that says DO NOT DISTURB in your door, people seem to respect that and bother you less.

It won't completely eliminate time vampires but it will lessen the possibility of getting distracted.

Action Guide:

Buy a "Do Not Disturb "Sign. Preferably, a sign that you can flip just like the ones you see on stores.

52 - Create a NO TO-DO List

What you don't do can be as important as what you do.

You may feel productive and focused because you're getting things done, but are you actually doing the right things?

Are you actually getting closer to your goals?

Or are you just masquerading?

Are you just making a fool of yourself? Telling yourself that you're finishing tasks and "improving", even though in reality, you're not really moving towards your goals

Action Guide:

1 - Be honest with yourself. Identify the tasks that are actually getting you closer to your desired results.

2 - Identify your NOT TO DO list. These are the things that you shouldn't do or the things that you should outsource to other people instead.

53 - Ditch the Open Door Policy

Look, I know that management gurus are still recommending an open door policy for a lot of executives.

Please, stop...just stop!

It doesn't work for most organization because it creates a culture of distraction.

How do you expect the business to thrive if the CEO of the company gets distracted every 15 minutes?

How do you expect people to get things done if a new request comes in unexpectedly?

Action Guide:

Ditch the open door policy.

It's stupid and it sucks... sorry, there's just no other way to say it.

54 - Be Genuinely Interested in What You Do

Nothing beats passion when it comes to focus. Being interested in what you're doing gets you through the tough times.

When you're interested and committed to what you're doing, focus is easy. You don't have to fight your inner demons to be passionate about what you're working on.

Now, I cannot tell you what you should be interested in. It's something that you have to figure out for yourself.

Action Guide:

Find something you enjoy doing, outsource the rest if you can.

It may take you months or years, but finding out what you're good at and what you're interested in is already a worthy endeavor in itself.

Conclusion

Focus is the currency of the future, and it's something that we have in all of us. We just have to cultivate the habit and practice of eliminating distractions.

Focus - It's something that we have control over, and it's something that we can build.

Are there random distractions everywhere? Of course. But that's why we have tons of ideas in this book to fight them.

What I recommend is that you try some of the ideas in this book – and discard the ones that you think are silly.

Focus on the ones that work for you and keep adding habits that you know are helping you gain focus in whatever you're doing.

I wish you all the best in your journey to a more productive and focused life.

-A.V. Mendez

A Special Request

If you enjoyed reading this action-packed, daily guide, I would like to request you to leave a short book review on Amazon.

I understand that reviewing a book takes some of your time and I want you to know that I really appreciate you as a reader.

I treat each review as precious and I would really appreciate you taking the time of your day to leave one on the book's Amazon page.

Thanks for reading this book and I will see you on the next one.

STOP PROCRASTINATION & INCREASE PRODUCTIVITY

60 Tricks on How to Improve Your Focus,
Time Management, Habits, Productivity and
Overall Ability to Get Things Done One Day at a Time

A.V. Mendez

TABLE OF CONTENTS

Part 3 - Motivation and How to Generate It ... *Page 158*

Day 21 - Know Your Whys

Day 22 - Use Your Envy to Your Advantage

Day 23 - Build Your Self-Discipline

Day 24 - Expand Your Will

Day 25 - Reward Yourself

Day 26 - "What Would This Look Like If It Was Easy?"

Day 27 - Find an Accountability Partner

Day 28 - Gun to Your Head Thinking

Day 29 - Track Each Other's Progress

Day 30 - Bet Some Money

Part 4 - Dealing with Procrastination ... *Page 170*

Day 31 - Manage Your Desktop

Day 32 - Manage Your Mobile Phone

Day 33 - Manage Your People

Day 34 - Organize Your Work Space

Day 35 - A Quiet Space = A Quiet Mind

Day 36 - Lessen Your Social Media Use

Day 37 - Trick Your Brain to Do Something

Day 38 - Develop a Sense of Urgency

Day 39 - The 20 Second Will Power Method

Day 40 - Know the Difference Between Important Vs. Urgent

Part 5 - Habits to Build for Maximum Productivity ... *Page 188*

Day 41 - Write Down Your Ideas

Day 42 - Only Check Your Email Once a Day

Day 43 - Conduct Short But Effective Meetings

Day 44 - Use Your Calendar

Day 45 - Act "As If"

Day 46 - Walk Outside

Day 47 - Stretching Your Body

Day 48 - Drink Water Every 2 Hours

Day 49 - Drink a Green Juice or Smoothie First Thing in the Morning

Day 50 - Pray, Meditate, or Connect

Day 51 - Time Blocking

Day 52 - Work Chunking

Day 53 - Batch Your Tasks

Day 54 - Set Your Appointments in Advance

Day 55 - Know When to Delegate

Day 56 - Sleep Better

Day 57 - The Slight Edge

Day 58 - Identify Your Bad Habits and Change Them

Day 59 - Take a Nap

Day 60 - Set a Not-To-Do List

OTHER BOOKS

Kindly visit the author's amazon page to check out other self-improvement books:

https://www.amazon.com/A.V.-Mendez/e/B00XU2UW5S/

Introduction

Procrastination, laziness, and unproductiveness.

In this book, I am going to help you deal with these without forcing you to do any unnecessary work.

Look, I understand your pain. I understand your dilemma. I was (and still at times), an unproductive mess! It feels like nothing seems to work for me. I was a procrastinator, I lacked focus, and I can't seem to start a project!

So what changed? How was I able to overcome my own laziness. How was I able to triple my productivity without doing more work than necessary?

Well, I started small. I started with 1 simple habit. Then I added another one, and another one... Today, I feel comfortable in saying that I am a productive - result oriented person.

And you can be the same!

But how?

In this book, I will teach you 60 small and actionable ideas that actually work. They may not be groundbreaking on each own, but combined, they will give you the best results imaginable.

You don't have to suffer from procrastination anymore. You don't have to force yourself to get up - because you can actually condition yourself to do so. You don't have to keep being distracted - with the ideas that I'm going to teach you, you can finally have focus in your life.

Now, you don't need any special skills or talents to double or triple your productivity. All I need from you is the desire to change and the commitment to take action.

If you have those 2 things, then productivity gets easier.

6 Sections of the Book

The book is divided into 6 parts. Each part will have 10 ideas that can help you in every aspect of productivity.

Part 1 - Setting Goals

The 1st one is about properly setting your goals. Without this, you will never be able to know whether what you're doing is actually worth it or not.

Part 2 - Building Your Focus Muscle

The next part is about building your focus muscle. It's about practicing how to become more focused.

Part 3 - Motivation and How to Generate It

Most of us don't have the motivation to start, work and finish something. We get too lazy, too tired, and too uninterested to do anything. This section will give you 10 ideas you can use to improve your motivation and force you to take action on a daily basis.

Part 4 - Dealing with Procrastination

The 4th part goes into detail about the strategies you can use to eliminate, avoid, and fight procrastination. After this section, you will understand yourself more and be able to generate motivation on a regular basis.

Part 5 - Habits to Build for Maximum Productivity

We don't want to rely on willpower alone. We need to build habits that we can do effortlessly. In this section, I'm going to show you what these habits are and how it can help you get more things done.

Part 6 - Strategies for Maximum Productivity

These are the action-focused strategies that you can use almost instantly to maximize your productivity.

Follow all of these lessons and watch the result for yourself. Within 30-60 days, you'll be shocked at how huge of an effect they can have on your productivity.

Okay, ready to double your productivity? 3 2 1, Let's go!

Part 1
Goal Setting

Day 1 - Your Definite Major Purpose

Think of it this way. Your definite major purpose is the thing that you want to do for the rest of your life. It's something that makes waking up in the morning worth it. It's something that you strive for long-term. It's something that you want to do and achieve for the rest of your life. It's something bigger than yourself. It's also the reason why, even failure after failure, you still get back up and try again.

Now, I understand that most people feel lost and they haven't had an inkling of their Definite Major Purpose (DMP). That's alright. Because it's something that you search for. It's something that sometimes, you just stumble upon.

So why is it important? Why is it that you need to find it?

Because if you never try to, you will live the rest of your life asking the question "what if?"

Your DMP will serve as the GPS for your life. It can help you navigate roads unbeknownst to you. It can help you find the path that leads to happiness and fulfillment.

It also makes you productive as heck! Why? Because knowing what path to take also means knowing what actions to do on a daily or weekly basis. It means you'll know exactly where you are going. And in productivity, you want to know exactly the outcomes you are aiming for - so you can be effective and efficient at the same time.

How to Find Your DMP

Here are 3 ways to find your DMP.

1 - Put Yourself Out There

If you have no clue where to get started, then you just have to put yourself out there. You need to do anything and try things that you haven't done before.

You can start with your potential hobbies and interest. Things like sports, entertainment, business, or anything that inspires you.

2- Scratch Your Own Itch

Do you have a problem that you want to solve? Do you have problems where solutions aren't easily accessible? Then maybe you need to scratch your own itch and find the solution for it yourself.

3 - Look at the World's Problem

This is a bigger picture thinking. If you've done everything, and your successful but unfulfilled, then maybe you need to help more people solve their problems. Look at the world's biggest problems and solve them. Choose one industry and dedicate your life to solving that crisis.

Action Guide:

1 - Don't be afraid to put yourself out there. Try different things and see what clicks for you. Yes, you will probably hate some of the things you will try, but at least, you'll now know what you don't want to do. Here's a quick exercise. Make a list of all the

things that you want to try. Riding motorcycles, paragliding, starting a business idea, etc.

Day 2 - Have Your Vision of the Future

If your DMP is what you want to do, having a vision for the future is something that you want to have and become. It's the end goal. It's something that is almost impossible to achieve in your mind.

Your vision is the change that you want to have. What exactly is your life going to be 30-40 years from now?

This may seem too "big picture" to be related to productivity, but trust me, this will serve as the foundation of your long-term success.

Look, we don't just want to be productive on the short-term. We want to be able to achieve greater things in life.

The purpose of "Part 1 - Setting Goals" is to give you the right direction in life. I don't want you to be productive on things that you hate doing. I don't want you to "get things done" and end up lonely as heck.

So what is your vision of the future?

Focus on yourself first (and there's nothing wrong with that).

What kind of house do you want to live in?

How big is it? What does it look like?

What car do you drive?

A Ferrari? A Lambo? A Honda? It doesn't matter what you drive. The most important part is you love having it.

What are the places you go to?

Do you like to visit New York, Paris, the Islands of the Philippines? Do you even travel at all?

What does your average day look like?

Do you work every day on things that you love doing? Are you retired earlier than most of your peers?

Action Guide:

Start writing a one-page vision for your future.

Just write what you want to have. It doesn't matter where you are in life right now. Broke, barely getting by, has 3 jobs, currently starting a business or whatever.

The most important stuff is that you have a general vision of what you want your life to look like.

Having this vision helps in reminding you of what you want to gain in the future. Look at it as if it's the sun. We know that the sun always rises in the east. So if you want to go east, just look at the sun and follow the trail. It's the same with your vision, follow that goal and keep on walking straight at it - eventually, you'll end up on the place where you want to go to.

Day 3 - Mindmap Your Plan

Now we go into more tactical stuff.

A mindmap is basically a program that helps you map out a goal, a lesson, a topic or pretty much anything you want. It is an organizational tool that you can use to help you see the whole picture and the steps needed to achieve a certain goal at the same time.

By having a mindmap, you won't get lost in the process and you'll know exactly what part of the plan you are currently implementing.

So where can you use your mindmap? When does it make sense to create one?

1 - Business plan

A business plan requires planning. You need quite a lot of information that you can use before you can finish one. What you can do is create a mindmap of ideas that you need to put in your business plan. Doing this helps you in organizing the ideas and the steps needed for you to finish your business plan.

2 - Writing books

A book needs lots of ideas for you to create it. Start by brainstorming ideas and put them on a mindmap. The goal of the mindmap is to put your thoughts into a written structure. Once you have those ideas scattered in the mind map, you can now arrange them by its logical steps.

3 - Organization member's map

Do you have a big company? Then you need to map out the CEO, chairman, president, managers, and other employees.

Doing this also helps in knowing the importance of each member since it gives the hierarchical structure of who is to be responsible for certain tasks and goals.

4 - Learning

If you want to learn, then you have to take notes. For some people, having an organized note based on a mindmap helps in remembering the lessons that you learned from what you studied. This eliminates overwhelm since you only have to open the maps that you want to review. A mindmap also helps in easily finding the topic that you want to review - thus, giving you more time and more productivity.

5 - Daily tasks

You can also use a mindmap in your daily tasks. Instead of a list, you can create a map of things that you need to do for the day or the week.

Action Guide:

1 - Download any free or paid mindmap that you want to use. I recommend Xmind, freemind or MindMeister.

2 - Start by mapping an idea that you want to implement. Let's say that you want to make an extra $2,000 per month as a freelance content writer. Ask yourself, what are the steps that you need to take in order to achieve that goal?

Put those steps in the mindmap and follow it until you hit your goal. The more details you put, the better the results will be.

3 - When you create your first mindmap, try to make it as simple as possible. Don't worry about the designs or colors. Just focus on the ideas first because they're the most important part of the mind mapping process.

Day 4 - Define the Steps Needed to Achieve Your Goals

Once you have a vision or a goal, it'll now be easier for you to narrow down the steps needed for you to achieve what you want.

Let's say that you want to write a book. You can use a mindmap to put the steps that you need to take to finish the book. Then put as many details as you can so you won't get lost in the process.

Knowing what you need to do means you'll spend less time thinking and more time taking action.

Defining these steps doesn't mean everything is going to be perfect. You will likely adjust and change some parts of the plan. But having that core steps that you need to take will serve as part of the foundation of being more productive - effective and efficient at the same time.

The reason a lot of people are unproductive is that they have no idea what they should be doing on a daily basis. They lack the detailed plan that will take them to the promised land. They do not know the steps that they need to take in order to go from where they are to where they want to be.

Let's change that! Here is how you can plan your goals and achieve them as fast as possible.

Action Guide:

1- Identify the logical order

Every goal has some kind of logical process that needs to happen so you can achieve them.

So for example, if you want to write a book, then there are things that you need to do in order to finish it.

You have to research your topic, come up with a title, create the outlines, write the book, design a book cover, and publish the book. Each of these steps has more sub-topics under them that you need to do in order to finish the whole thing.

Identify those steps and put them on a mindmap.

2- Research

The next step is the research process. Every goal needs some kind new information that you need to have for you to achieve it. The research will depend on what you want.

Do you want to become a writer? Then you probably have to learn how to outline a book. You need to have the discipline to write every day. And you need to learn how to publish a book. All these things must be done, for you to finish the project - and if you have no idea how to do them, then you will never achieve your goal of writing a book. You need to research the steps properly so you can be sure that you have adequate knowledge to actually finish what you want to achieve.

3 - Identify the resources

The next step is to identify the resources needed to achieve the goal. Again, this will depend on the topic.

The resources are the tools that you need in order to implement your plan. They also help in making you be more efficient in doing your tasks.

4 - Start implementing through results-focused action

Results focused actions are the things that you do that brings in the result. If you are a consultant, then client outreach could be your "result focused action." Although studying online courses to become a better consultant is important, at the end of the day, the result will still come from client outreach. In this case, you should spend more time on client outreach more than studying about consulting.

Did you get it? Focus on the stuff that will bring in the result [the profit]. These are the actions that will lead to a faster and better outcome.

Day 5 - Know the Tools (Resources) Needed to Achieve Your Goals

Achieving a goal needs more than just a plan. It doesn't just need motivation and willpower. It also needs some tools that can help you to become more efficient in the process. The better tools you have, the more you'll be able to maximize your results.

There are different types of tools (resources) needed to achieve a certain goal. These resources will depend on your industry or goal. I cannot possibly give you the exact tools you need since we all have different goals. What I can give you is a list of resources needed that you could use in general - in business, sports, entertainment, and other industries.

TOP RESOURCES

Capital

Most business ventures require some kind of capital for you to start it. There are lots of ways to raise money.

You can bootstrap, get it from family and friends, capital venture, angel investors, bank loans and private equity.

Energy

When I say energy, what I mean is your personal physical energy. It's something that you need to have in order to perform at the maximum level.

Without it, you won't be able to achieve your goals. Without it, you'll fail, you'll procrastinate, and you'll quit.

Software

The software helps us in finishing tasks faster. Find a software that can help you solve your problems. Some will be paid and some will be free. As long as you need the software, then what you pay for it is worth the price.

People

Another important resource that you need to have are people. People are the hardest to manage since we can be unpredictable. Yet it's something that you probably need in order to grow your business or achieve a goal that you want to get.

For most companies/ventures, people will always be the most important part of the game. The people are the ones making everything work. The people are the ones controlling the machine. Without its people, then the organization is considered nothing of value.

Action Guide:

1 - Know the goal that you want to achieve.

2 - Identify the tools needed for you to maximize your results. Again, these tools will depend on what you're aiming for. Different goals and industries will have different tools. Your job is to find the best ones that you can use to finish your tasks.

3 - Know what you really need. Do you need capital, energy, software or people?

Day 6 - Know Your Priorities

Here's one mindset shift that saved me hundreds if not thousands of hours of useless work over the years.

"Setting priorities is the priority."

That's right, if you want to be productive, then you have to set your priorities right. In fact, setting the priorities should be your number one priority.

Every day, you should have a set of task that you want and need to do. And every day, you should have 1 or 2 important tasks that you should do first. Usually, these are the hardest ones to do. These are the ones that require a lot of brain power. They don't necessarily have to be physically hard. If it's very taxing to the brain, and if it requires you to think harder than usual - then I would consider it hard.

Let's say that you are an FB Ads Consultant/Freelancer.

Your number 1 priority is getting clients. That's how you pay the bills and that's how you earn a living. Getting clients usually requires you to talk to potential clients. In this case, your number 1 priority is to talk to at least 1 or 2 potential clients in the morning. As long as you're doing this every day, then you are more likely to achieve your income goal. Every other task like running FB ads, designing some logo and anything that doesn't relate much to client outreach should be done after your task #1.

Whatever your profession is, whatever your goals are - there will always be 1 or 2 tasks that will stand out. These are the hardest yet the most important ones to do.

As long as you do these things consistently, the chance of you hitting your goals is going to be great.

Your most important task should have a direct effect on your desired outcome.

For example, your goal is to learn how to raise money for your startup. Creating your business plan, improving your prototype, designing your pitch deck... these are all crucial tasks. But nothing is more important than reaching out to potential investors. NOTHING. Why? Because your goal is to raise money and all of these other stuff won't matter if you have no one to pitch to.

It's the same with every other industry, niche, tasks, etc.

Focus on 1 or 2 tasks that will bring in the results.

Action Guide:

1 - Study your own business or job. Look at the top 2 tasks that you should do in order to get the desired results.

2 - Prioritize your tasks by starting with the hardest one to do. After finishing your main task, every other task for the remainder of the day would now feel very doable. You already did the hardest task, the next few ones will now be easier and faster to finish.

Day 7 - Plan Your Year and Months

It's great to measure your success on a yearly basis. It's easier to compare your achievements year by year compared to per month or per day.

It's a good test for you and your business because the year consists of a lot of ups and downs.

There are good months, and there are bad months. And by having the yearly data to compare to, you'll be able to see your progress on a higher level.

So when I say plan your year, what does it exactly mean? How do you even do that?

Planning your year means looking at different parts of your business. Your plan may consists of production, management, marketing promotions, expansion, etc.

So it will all depend on your business or profession.

Let's say that you are an online course creator.

What are the courses that you will launch this year? What are the promotions that you are going to run? You should create a year-long plan that will help you promote your online courses and you should look at the promotion as a whole.

In this case, you will have a promotion from January to December. Obviously, each promo will differ from one another.

For January, you can promote your online course, and for February, you can promote your book. Another thing to look at is the medium. In January, you can use email as the main promotion medium. On February, you can use videos.

Whatever you do, there should be a plan of action that you will do on a monthly basis.

Every month, you will have some specific goal that you need to hit. All of these goals should add up to your yearly goals and you should be able to know what to do in order to achieve them.

Action Guide:

1 - Set a yearly goal for all aspects of your life - physical, emotional, mental and financial.

2 - Create a monthly plan that you need to implement that will lead you to achieving your goals.

3 - Use a calendar and put all the things that you will do for every month.

4 - Put an X mark for every month where you actually finish the monthly tasks you set for yourself.

5 - Learn to adjust on the fly. Not everything will work for you. Write the worst case scenario for your project. "If this happens, I would still consider it a success." What does it look like for you? What does success mean in relation to your project?

Day 8 - Plan Your Week

Now that you have a month by month goal that you need to do, the next step is to create a weekly plan of execution.

What are the things that you need to do on a weekly basis that can help you achieve your monthly goals? What are the steps that you need to do so you can say that your week or your month is a success?

Again, this will all depend on what you want to achieve.

Let's suppose that you're a creative director who wants to create 1 short film per month. For this month's goal, you want to finish the shoot for your movie called "Where Are You Water?"

To finish the film, there are certain tasks that needs to get done on a daily and weekly basis. Before you set your daily task, you have to know your weekly deadlines first.

In your goal, your week could look something like this:

Week 1 - Crafting the Script, Casting the Actors
Week 2 - Filming
Week 3 - Editing
Week 4 - Marketing and Promotion

In this case, you'll know exactly what needs to happen for you to achieve your monthly goal of finishing a short film.

You need a script and actors, you need to film it, you need to edit it and then promote it.

The time frame may differ based on your goals, but all tasks will have some kind of logical order for you to finish them.

Let me give another example. Let' say that your goal for this month is to create an ebook lead magnet that you can give to your audience.

To create that ebook, you need to do the following:

-Research your topic
-Identify your main topic
-Outline your book
-Write the short ebook
-Edit the book
-Format the interior layout
-Create a book cover
-Create a landing page to get their email address
-Promote the ebook lead magnet through Facebook ads

Next, you're going to have to create a weekly goal that you need to achieve.

For example.

For week 1, you need to finish the following:

-Research your topic
-Identify your main topic
-Outline your book

For week 2, you need to finish this:

-Write the short ebook

For week 3-4, you need to finish all these tasks:

-Edit the book
-Format the interior layout
-Create a book cover
-Create a landing page to get their email address
-Promote the ebook lead magnet through Facebook ads

Having this weekly outline for your goal makes the process easier for you.

You won't get lost doing random stuff because you have a goal that is guiding you throughout the whole process.

Having this weekly goal that needs to be met is crucial in achieving your monthly and yearly goals.

If you are hitting your weekly and monthly goals, then there's a great chance that you'll also hit your bigger, long-term goals.

Action Guide:

1 - Create a weekly plan of action. What are the things that you need to finish this week? These should be things that will have a direct effect on your monthly and yearly goal.

If a task is moving you forward in a measurable manner, then you are doing it right.

Day 9 - Create Your To-Do List the Day Before

Every night, I make sure to create my to-do list first before I sleep. This helps me become more productive in the morning. Instead of thinking about what I'm going to do, I already have a set of activities that I need to do for the next day.

This saves me lots of time and energy that I can use on my most important tasks.

Instead of coming up with ideas to do in the morning, creating one the day before makes you go straight to the action part.

Another thing that you can do is to create your to-do list good for 3-5 days.

Let's say that you are a writer and an online course marketer.

Here's what a sample to-do list could look like for you:
Weekly Goal #1: To finish writing my short eBook and create a book cover

Weekly Goal #2: Promote my online course

Monday - To-Do List

Write 1,000 words 9am-12nn

Create mock-up for the book cover 1-3pm

Write and Post a value based post on Facebook - 3-5pm

Tuesday - To-Do List

Write 1,000 words 9am-12nn

Review your first 1,000 words - 1-2pm

Create a 5-minute video content related to the online course I'm promoting - 2-3pm

Wednesday- To-Do List

Write 1,000 words 9am-12nn

Review your first 1,000 words - 1-2pm

Create a 5-minute video content related to the online course I'm promoting - 2-3pm

Action Guide:

1 - Create a detailed to-do list that is specific and has a deadline.

2 - Do not overcommit, create more than 5 tasks on your t-do list.

3 - Always do your most important task.

4 - Focus on creating quality work. It pays better in the long-term.

5 - Create your list in advance for Monday to Friday (if the tasks you set are predictable enough to do on to regular basis).

Day 10 - What Does Your Perfect Day Looks Like?

Now let's get into slightly weird territory. I'm going to ask you what your perfect day looks like.

In a way, your industry, job, business or profession doesn't matter. Whatever you do in life, this will still apply to you.

Now, why am I asking you what a perfect day looks like for you?

Because I don't just want you to become productive.

I also want you to be happy and productive at the same time.

By having an idea of what your perfect day looks like, you won't be part of the population who found a way to be "productive" yet ended up being sad and depressed.

Now, I do understand that on our way to success, we are going to have to do some things that we found to be uncomfortable, unpleasant and shi*ty.

But humor me for a second here and just stick to my suggestion.

Action Guide:

1 - Create a one-page manifesto of what your average day would look like. What does an average (but still awesome) day would look like for you? What foods will you eat? What time will you wake up? Who would you wake up to? What are the things that you are going to do?

2 - I recommend that you create an account of what happens every hour.

Here's a short example of an Average Day One-Pager Exercise:

I wake up at 6am. I kiss my wife and my kids and thank God for all the blessings the I have. I make breakfast for my family and I go to the gym for 1 hour. Once I returned, I feel super refresh and now ready to work on my coaching business. I talk to my clients from 8am-11am and most of my work is now finished. By 11am to 1pm, I spend the time either writing or reading. I have a healthy lunch with my wife and we talk about random stuff. I start working again on my business from 2pm-4pm. I enjoy every minute of it and I wouldn't have it any other way. From 4 pm onwards, I have a free schedule and I can do whatever I want. Play with my kids, watch a movie, read a book, talk to a friend, even work on my business If I feel like it. I sleep at around 10pm to 6am and I always wake up with a smile on my face.

3 - Start and finish your Average Day one-pager. This will help remind you of the things that you value. It's not enough that you are productive. You also have to be happy and fulfilled at the same time.

4 - I understand that this may be a corny exercise but I still recommend that you do it. You have nothing to lose. All I want for you is for you to have an idea of what life you want to live. By doing this, you'll be able to make decisions based on fulfillment rather than solely on financial success.

Part 2
Building Your
Focus Muscle

Day 11 - Control Interruptions

Interruptions are everywhere. It's something that is almost impossible to avoid. Interruptions are things like your desktop and mobile notifications, social media, outside noises, other people, e-mail and many more.

We can never really eliminate interruptions. Sometimes, they just come out of nowhere. The best thing we can do is to control how much interruptions are coming our way.

You can put a "Do Not Disturb" sign on your office door. You can ask people in advance not to bother you at a certain time. You can turn off your notifications. You can put your phone in the other room.

These are the things we have control over.

When it comes to interruptions, the name of the game is preemptive solutions. Try not to let the interruptions happen in the first place. Do the things that will lessen the chance of distractions.

Now, no matter what you do, there will always be some kind of unexpected interruptions. I have no idea where it will come from but believe me when I say, it'll come and it'll try to take you away from your work. When this happens, all you can do is to fight it. To be patient and choose to focus on your work instead.

Action Guide:

1 - Know the commons interruptions that you get every day. Is it your dogs? Your cat? Your officemate? A friend? Your social media notifications?

2 - Whatever or whoever they are, prepare yourself by doing something that will help prevent this interruption from happening. Find the best solution. Focus first on prevention. Then if it passes through the preemptive solution, prepare for what you have to do instead.

3 - Make a list of the usual distractions that you get on a daily basis. Start finding a solution for the ones that almost always happen.

4 - Remember the saying "Prevention is better than cure."

Day 12 - Do Not Multitask

I do not need to mention hundreds of studies for you to believe that multitasking doesn't work. You know it in your heart of hearts that doing task simultaneously is just not an effective use of your time.

Sure, you might feel productive for a second there, but at the end of the day, you know that the quality of your work suffers every time you multitask.

You know that the name of the game is focus. You know that you should only focus on one task at a time.

Just because you finished 2 tasks at the same time doesn't mean you're a productive person. Always remember that the quality of your output is as important as finishing all your tasks.

Another thing to notice is the amount of browsing you do when you're doing your task.

Let's say that you are writing your book. Do not open Facebook, YouTube or any other website or application while you are writing. You will find it harder to refocus and get back to that mindset of writing.

When you start browsing other applications or website, you will need a lot of time to get your focus back on the main task. Personally, it takes me around 10 minutes of mindless browsing and thinking before I can get back at my task.

This waste a lot of time that I could've use on writing instead.

So focus on your main task as much as you can. The browsing, the distractions - they're just not worth it.

Action Guide:

1 - Stop multitasking

2 - Do your own experiment. Do one task at a time and do 2 tasks at another time. Compare the quality of your work and compare the hours it took you to finished the projects. 9 times out of 10, you'll be happier at the experiment where you focus on one task at a time.

Day 13 - Use Two Monitors

I've never been a believer of 2 monitors.

I always thought that it was just for traders.

I thought that they were a waste of time and only for people who want to look smart on Facebook and Instagram.

Surprise, surprise!

It's actually a really helpful tool that can save you lots of time and help you focus on your task.

It helps when you need to look at your research more often. It helps in tracking changing information. It helps in making sure that you don't have a billion tabs opened in your computer.

If you use it wisely, it can actually be one of the best investments you will ever make in terms of focus and productivity.

Action Guide:

1 - Search for the best dual monitors that fits your budget.

2 - Buy a second screen with no less than 15 inches of real estate.

3 - Use your first screen for doing your main task. Use the second screen for complementary tasks. Stuff like research materials, information you need to look at and moving parts in your business that you need to keep track of.

Day 14 - Building Your Concentration Muscle

Building your concentration is like building your muscle. At first, you probably have not much of it. Then you start lifting, eating right, then lift again...then you repeat the process over and over again.

One day, you'll just notice that you're already at less than 7% body fat. Down from your original 15% body fat 6 months ago.

When it comes to your concentration, you need to practice building it over time. You cannot rely on willpower alone. You cannot rely on having concentration only when "I feel like it."

By building your concentration muscle, you don't have to be inconsistent in your ability to focus. Having the concentration muscle allows you to be the best you at all times. What I found is there are some activities that really help you do this....

Action Guide:

... Here are some concentration games you can play with your friends. You not only build focus but you also have fun at the same time!

1 - Crossword
2- Jigsaw puzzle
3 - Wire concentration game
4- Rubiks cube
5 - Trivia
6 - Pass the message game

Here are some non-game concentration building exercises you can do:

1 - Reading fiction or nonfiction

2 - Doodle something

3 - Meditation

4 - Sit still in a chair and do nothing. Leave your phone somewhere you cannot easily get it.

Day 15 - Take Short Breaks

We now live in a world where hustle is glorified and rest is laughed at. It's as if resting and taking a break isn't allowed anymore. It's as if it's a shame if you only work 8 hours instead of 12.

I want you to destroy this mindset. Your rest is also as important as the work itself.

I recommend that you do short breaks after every 50-60 minutes of work.

Follow the Pomodoro technique of working in time chunks.

I found that working for 50 minutes and resting for 10 works the best for me. I just repeat this process over and over again, but I take more rest after the 3rd hour. Usually, my Pomodoro would look like this:

50 minutes work, 10 minutes rest
50 minutes work, 10 minutes rest
50 minutes work, 25 minutes rest

40 minutes work, 10 minutes rest
40 minutes work, 15 minutes rest

I reduce my work time and increase my rest time as the day goes by. Why? Because I usually have the most energy during mornings. By around lunchtime, the need for rest becomes more important.

We're not just focusing on the time here. We're also focusing on the quality of our work.

Action Guide:

1 - Have the mindset that rest is needed if you are to be the most effective version of yourself.

2 - Follow the Pomodoro technique in all your tasks. Make sure that you rest for at least 5-10 minutes for every hour of work that you do. Then 10-15(or 20) minutes rest after every 3 hours of work.

Day 16 - Listen to Music That Makes You Productive

There are different types of music that can make you more productive. Music like classical music, rock, country or anything that calms your mind.

Let's go straight to what works.

Thing is, it will be different for everybody.

For some, classical music works best. For some, it'll be pop songs. So there's no one correct answer here. The key is to test out different types of music.

Here are the strategies (and music type) that I've tried before:

1 - Mozart

Classical music has been proven to increase concentration and focus. This is the first one that I would recommend you try.

2 - 1 song on repeat

Listening to one song over and over again until it fades away into the background is one of the best one you can try.

3 - Rock

Rock music works best for me whenever I'm doing something boring. Usually, I'll play rock music if I'm doing administrative tasks. This makes the process a little more fun for me.

4 - Country

I also love listening to country music if I just want to relax and have a laid back type of work.

5 - Random

For some, the type of music doesn't really matter. It could be rap, country, classical, or whatever - the type of music doesn't really affect their productivity that much.

Action Guide:

1 - Choose a type of music that works best for you. Here's my initial recommendation.

For creative tasks, choose classical music.

For admin stuff, choose rap, pop or rock.

Day 17 - The Power of Noise Canceling Headphones

Is this the greatest invention of all time?

Hmmm.. probably not.

But I can't count how many times I've thanked the Gods of headphones for inventing it. It saved me so much time - from distractions and potential interrupters.

I almost always use noise-canceling headphones whenever I'm working on something important.

If it's going to help me achieve my goal, then that task is important and you will always find me wearing my own NCH.

I love wearing NCH because I get fewer distractions from people who would've approached me otherwise if I'm not wearing it. Me wearing an NCH means I'm busy. It shows the people around me that I'm not to be bothered at that time.

If you work in an office, you have to train the people around you to notice that, you wearing an NCH means you don't want to be bothered as much as possible.

If you work at home or coffee shops, you will be able to avoid the noise of the environment, thus helping you avoid distractions.

Using a noise canceling headphone is definitely one of my favorite hacks for improving my productivity and focus.

Action Guide:

1 - Go buy your first noise-canceling headphones. The sweet spot, in my opinion, is the $150-$200 mark.

2 - Here are some of my recommendations:

Sennheiser HD 4.50 BTNC - $140

Audio-Technica ANC9 - $120

Sony MDRZX110NC - $30

Bose QuietComfort 25 - $180

Plantronics Backbeat Pro 2 - $135

3 - Don't get too hang up on choosing your NCH. Just buy what you can afford or better yet, test one first and then return it if doesn't match your ear size and sound preference.

Day 18 - Use Memorizing Techniques to Keep Your Brain Sharp

My mom used to tease me about how my brain power won't increase because I always ask her about all the little things that I could've - think, done, and find myself.

I always asked for her assistance on something. Today, I now realize the value of thinking for yourself. The value of practicing stuff to keep our brain sharp.

One of the things that will have a big impact on your ability to get things done is your capacity to keep your brain as sharp as possible.

In order to get things done and be the best that you can be, you need your brain to be at 100%. You need it to be sharp and fast. You need to make your brain ready for any problems you may encounter.

I found that memorization techniques work well in helping me keep my brain active and sharp.

It's like the more we used it, the better it gets.

Action Guide:

1 - Here are some memorization techniques I recommend that you do:

A - Memorize a playing card.

B - Dictate at least 10 of your closest friends.

C - Make a list of all the movies you watched this year. Then memorize all of them.

D- Hand copy a list

E - Use chunking

F - Use mnemonics

Check out this article for more information about chunking and mnemonics:

https://zapier.com/blog/better-memory/

2 - Choose one or two that you can do every week. Then change it the next week so you can try out as many different exercises as you can.

Day 19 - Unplug Yourself

Once every 30 days, I have my own "Unplug Day" where I do not use any electronic device at all. That means 24 hours of just doing anything that has nothing to do with electronics.

It could be reading a book, writing on a notebook, having some kind of one-day quick vacation, talking to my family, having fun with my friends, etc.

I recommend that you do this Unplug Day at least once a month. This will help you recharge your battery. It'll also give you enough time to think about the more important things in life.

This one-day reflection somehow gives me a sense of renewed energy.

Action Guide:

Have your own unplug day and do something that doesn't require you to use any electronic device. A device like smartphones, tablets, laptop or anything that will connect you to the outside world through the internet. Here are some activities you can do:

1 - Reading
2 - Writing
3 - Biking
4 - Riding a motorcycle
5 - Going to the beach
6 - Having long drives with your partner

7 - Playing with your kids

8 - Watching a live sport game

Day 20 - Track Your Progress

Every week, I spend at least 1 hour just looking back at my progress - in life, business, emotional health, physical health, and mental health. I try to make sure that I'm moving towards my goals.

Am I finishing my daily tasks?

Do I feel like I am growing as a person?

Am I learning a lot of new things?

Am I being challenged?

My goal every week is to make sure that I am growing, that I am improving.

Because if not, then that only means that what I'm doing isn't working. That means I have to change my plan and change my action at the same time.

Track your progress every week. Remember that if you're not moving forward, then that means that you're not inching towards the goals that you set for yourself.

Action Guide:

1 - Set a specific date and time on the weekends where you'll track your progress and write about tasks you achieved, things you learned and your plans for the next week. Treat this task as a "must-do" kind of task. It's something that you have to do every

week to make sure that you're not losing track of your goal. It's something that you need to keep on doing to make sure that you're getting closer to your dreams.

Part 3
Motivation and
How to Generate It

Day 21 - Know Your Whys

Knowing your why makes you move, literally speaking. It makes you keep going when it seems like there's nothing going right in your life.

Your why keeps you grounded. It helps you remember why you got started in the first place. It helps a lot in whatever you're trying to achieve. Your why will always have a big impact on your success?

Without your whys, you would've probably quit a long time ago. Without your whys your success may not be as meaningful as you thought it would be.

Your why is the reason why you do what you do.

So what is your why?

Do you want to buy a Ferrari? Do you want to have money for retirement? Do you want to pay your kid's college tuition fee? Do you want to feel fulfillment?

Action Guide:

Whatever your why is, make sure that you write it down and read it at least once a week.

You want to always have a reminder of why you're doing what you're doing. The harder the goal is to attain, the deeper the why you should have.

Day 22 - Use Your Envy to Your Advantage

Just like any other person, I used to feel envy with other people's success. The only difference is I now learned how to use envy and turn it into motivation.

Whenever I feel envious of someone, I acknowledge how I feel. Then I ask myself, how can I use this feeling to my advantage?

Then I turn that feeling of envy and disappointment to motivation by using it as a chip on my soldier.

Some colleague earned so and so? "Cool, good for him." Then I tell myself, "If he can do it, I can do it too" – this gives me the feeling of motivation to do shit. This gives me the fire to take action. Instead of feeling envious of my friends or other people – I start being happy for them and then use that initial knee jerk reaction to my advantage.

It's a win-win. I become genuinely happy for others and I also give myself the motivation to make things happen.

I'm not exactly sure whether that's good practice to have or not – all I know is it works for me and I like the results that it gives.

Action Guide:

The next time you feel envy towards another's success, immediately acknowledge that feeling and then turn it into motivation. Use the strategy that I mentioned above.

Focus on how you can use that motivation instead of focusing on how others have what you don't.

Day 23 - Build Your Self-Discipline

Your self-discipline is what would separate you from other people. Your discipline is what will dictate your success.

Are you willing to wake up early every day to go to work and be the most productive version of yourself?

Are you willing to work 12 hour days especially if you're just starting out in business?

Are you willing to practice on your game even on weekends?

Are you willing to do these things? Or would you rather just watch Netflix?

Your action has to match your ambition. You have to actually do the hard stuff - not just talk about it.

Action Guide:

1 - Create small habits that build self-discipline.

Habits like waking up early, exercising, stretching, meditating and drinking water every day.

Start with something easy. Something that you can do in just a few minutes a day.

Day 24 - Expand Your Will

Your will is your desire to achieve great things. Your will is what allows you to dream big and push yourself against the limits.

If you do not have the will to succeed, then "hard work" won't solve the problem. - because you won't work hard in the first place.

In order to build your will, you have to find out your whys. You have to know what you want to achieve.

If you will only grasp the midpoint of your potential, then that's where you will end up.

You will to succeed, your dog in the fight has to be there. If not, then there's no point in making yourself "productive." You will never be able to move because you have no reason to do sh*t anyway.

Action Guide:

Build your will by doing the following:

1 – Make a list of your whys. Why do you do what you do?

2 - Know what are the businesses, sports or topics you want to work around with.

3 - Know who are the people whom you are doing all of these for. It could be your wife, parents, kids, friends, or even yourself.

Day 25 - Reward Yourself

Learn to celebrate your wins. It doesn't matter if it's just a $200 first consulting deal or a big $200,000 project. Learn to appreciate what you received by celebrating what you have.

A lot of people do not enjoy the process because there's always something to catch. Closed a $500 deal? "Ok, I need to go for $1,000 now." Closed that $1,000 deal? "That's not enough, we need more" - the cycle repeats itself over and over again. And you end up unhappy and unproductive.

Action Guide:

1 - Make sure that you match your reward with your achievement. If you won a game, then go get yourself a nice dinner. If you win the championship, then go party all night as much as you can.

You can't close a $300 deal and just party and get drunk all night. Unless you're banking hundreds of thousands of dollars, then that's the only time you can give yourself permission to party. Even then, you still have to be careful about the reward you give to yourself.

Make sure that it's not too extravagant.

Match your reward with your level of achievement.

Day 26 - "What Would This Look Like If It Was Easy?"

Often, we tend to complicate things. Although I understand that the world isn't just black and white, the truth is we still tend to overcomplicate lots of the things that we do.

I write advertisements for a living. Sometimes, I have the tendency to overthink every word, every sentence and every design that goes into the ads. But nothing can be further from the truth. If you want to have an ad that works, then the only real way to know is to test it! So instead of spending hundreds of hours perfecting the ad, create a basic one and then improve it as you get more data from the customers.

It's the same in most things that we do.

Make sure that you ask the question "What Would This Look Like If It Was Easy?"... ask, and you shall find the answer.

Action Guide:

Look at the tasks that you set for yourself. Are you making it hard for yourself to finish them? Are you making things complicated?

If so, then it's time to change something. What would it look like if it was easy? This doesn't mean that you're looking for something that will magically do the work for you.

This only means that you want to finish faster while still doing it efficiently and effectively.

Day 27 - Find an Accountability Partner

One of the best-kept secret to increasing productivity and results is by having an accountability partner. An accountability partner is someone you can trust. Someone who will keep up with your progress. Someone who cares for you. This person is someone who will make sure that you walk the talk. This person is someone who is serious about helping you get better.

You can have an accountability partner when it comes to your finance, physical health, and even emotional and mental health.

Sometimes, these partners could be your doctor, psychiatrist, gym coach, etc.

Action Guide:

1 - Find your own accountability partner. It could be a friend, family member, or business partner. Try to choose someone who really cares about you.

2 - Bet something of value in exchange for not doing the tasks that you said you will do. Usually, a few dollars is enough to force me to move my butt. If I said that I'm going to give a partner $10 if I didn't go to the gym at least 2 times this week, then this gives me more incentive to take action. I don't want to lose that $10. Thus, I'm more likely to take action and follow the tasks I set for myself.

Day 28 - Gun to Your Head Thinking

I forgot where I heard this, but if you have a gun in your head and your teacher says "If you do not finish your essay in 2 hours, I will blow your heads off" - then this will surely make us take action. 99.9% of us would probably finish the essay. It doesn't matter if it's good or bad - the only important thing here is to finish it (as the teacher said).

In most of the things that you do, you can implement this mindset if you're really serious about it. This forces your brain to take action. This forces you to actually get started.

Action Guide:

1 - Pick a task that you are finding hard to do. Imagine that someone has a gun to your head and he will fire that bullet if you do not do your task.

Create this mindset of making sh*t happen and you will make sh*t happen.

2 - Pick something that you find hard to do. Things like writing, practicing, or anything that requires a lot of energy to do.

3 - Obviously, do not take this literally speaking. What I want you to get out of this is the mindset behind it - that you need to have a mindset based on taking action.

Day 29 - Track Each Other's Progress

Once you found an accountability partner,
you should also offer to track each other's progress.

It should be a win-win situation.

You should be able to help each other achieve
your dreams and goals.

Action Guide:

1 - Pick an accountability partner who also cares about self-development.

2 - Make sure that you care about each other's success.

3 - Pick someone who wouldn't judge you if you failed in some of the tasks you set for yourself.

4 - Pick one part of your lives that you can track every day or every week. It could be business, health, productivity or anything that makes your life better.

5 - Always encourage the other person to do the thing that he promised to do - because "this will be good for you" and "it will help you grow." (Say those exact words when encouraging someone).

Day 30 - Bet Some Money

Now let's take it to the next level.

Do you really want to increase your productivity and "walk to talk?"

Well, now it's time to bet some money.

I recommend that you bet money with your accountability partner. If you don't do the things that you say you would do, then he should keep the money that you bet.

To make this even more effective, you should have a timeline for doing these tasks. Till when should you do the task? How many hours do you need to finish it? Make the timeline clear.

In addition, make it as specific as possible. If the bet is about going to the gym, make sure that it's measurable. How many hours do you need to be there? What are you supposed to achieve? If you do that, then you win - you get to keep your money and you get closer to your goals.

Action Guide:

1 - Start betting small. Something like $2-10 is a good start.

2 - The harder the task is to do, the more money you should bet.

3 - Commit to a certain amount, a specific timeline and specific measurable results.

Part 4
Dealing with Procrastination

Day 31 - Manage Your Desktop

If you're like most people, then the desktop is where "the stuff happens." That's where you work is, that's where you open your important apps and file, and that's the window to your business or job.

Here's a way to categorize your desktop.

Folders - Work Files

Create folders for different tasks that you do.

Put them under "Work Files" and make sure that you put everything related to your work there.

Images/Videos

Separate your image and video files from your other files. Pictures and videos from vacation, vlogs, or any extra videos should be here.

You can also add a movie sub-folder if you have mp4 files that you want to watch.

Desktop Apps

All the desktop apps that you use on a daily basis should be on a folder called Desktop Apps. If you just have a few desktop apps that you constantly use, then put it on the home page window.

Delete Unused Files or Apps

If you have unused files or apps, then maybe it's time to consider that you delete them.

If you're still not sure about what to do with them, then transfer them on a flash drive or a hard drive.

New Admin

If you have a different set of work or tasks not related to each other, you can also create a new admin so you can focus on just one task. Doing this frees up your mind from distractions of other work or non-work related tasks.

Action Guide:

1 - The first step is to manage your folders. Arrange them by category so you won't have to get confused every time you search for an important file.

2 - Consider deleting apps and files that you don't use anymore. If you haven't opened that app or file for a year now, then you should consider deleting it already. Alternatively, you can also put the file on a hard drive.

Day 32 - Manage Your Mobile Phone

When it comes to mobile phone productivity, there are top 2 culprits that affect our productivity.

Games & Social Media

Games

Look, I understand. It's fun and it's addictive. It's something that can take your stress away. But too much of it can lead to unproductiveness, sleep deprivation and in some cases, even depression.

Take care of your mental health and increase your productivity by limiting your playing time. As fun as mobile games is, they're not really adding anything valuable in your life. Trust me, delete your mobile games for 7 days as a trial. 9 time out of 10, you'll find that you don't actually need them!

Social Media

Another big culprit is social media.

Facebook, Instagram, YouTube, and Twitter are the usual suspects.

If you check your phone every 30 minutes (or less), then something has to change. This isn't good for you and you know it too! Checking your social media constantly breaks focus. It allows you to drift off of the task that you should do. In addition, it makes you miserable because you always end up comparing yourself to what you see on social media (which is either too positive to be real or too negative to give attention to). Those Insta shots, Twitter rants, Facebook viral posts - they give us this instant hit of dopamine. Likes, comments, hearts, retweet, the whole 9 yards.

I would suggest that you read and learn more about this so you'll understand the consequences of us being fully engaged in social media but not in life.

Action Guide:

1 - Consider deleting your social media apps. Seriously, 99% of the time, you don't really need them on your phone.

2 - If you can't delete the apps, consider only using them for a maximum of two 30 minute rounds per day.

3 - Delete the mobile games on your phone. Do you want to play games or do you want to grow a business? Do you want to play mobile games while everyone that you admire is grinding and working their asses off? Shame.

Day 33 - Manage Your People

Productivity can't just be about you. It also has to be about the people around you. Unless you're a one-man team, then you have to manage other people to grow your business. You have to have people who are present - literally and figuratively speaking. You have to have people who are working at an effective and efficient rate. You have to have healthy people you can lean on to.

Here are the things you should manage about other people:

1 - Attendance

Make sure that they're always coming on time. And make sure that they are consistent in their attendance. It's hard to be productive as a team when someone is always on leave or late every week.

2 - Work Performance

At the end of the day, results are still all that matters. Are they doing their job? Are they getting results? If not, then you already know what to do.

3 - Mental health

An underrated aspect of people's work lives is their mental health. You have to check on your people, make sure that they are on the right mindset. Mental health is serious and it's something that you should spend money on.

4 - Physical Health

Unhealthy people bring bad results.

They have a hard time focusing on work. They can be irritable. And they can surely be a problem when it comes to the efficiency of work. Always encourage your team to live a healthy lifestyle. A physically healthy person tends to be consistent in his attendance, not likely to come late, be effective and efficient, and be healthier in terms of mental health.

Action Guide:

1 - Check these 4 things if you manage other people. Look at your employees or teammates and confirm whether they have problems with any of these or not.

Day 34 - Organize Your Work Space

Another source of distraction that you can easily avoid if you choose to is your workspace.

Do you have lots of stuff going on in your desk? Do you have a thousand pens lying around, mugs, your baseball cap, eraser, highlighters, etc.?

Ask yourself, do you really need to have these things on the table? Do you really use them on a daily basis? If not, then those things don't need to be there!

Action Guide:

It's time to clean your workspace.

Trash

Start with the trash. Are there any candy wrappers? Bottles of water? Or anything that you should have thrown out a long time ago?

Memorabilia

Look, I understand that you want to have a picture of your family in your workspace. It's a good motivational tool to have. But do you really need 7 different picture frames? Do you really need all the memorabilia in your desk? Or do you feel like you just need to put something on your desk?

Laptop and Nothing Else

This is a super minimalist set up so it might or might not be right for you. A cluttered desk is a sign of a cluttered mind.
And I do recommend that you try putting your laptop and nothing else on your desk.

Try it for 2 weeks. See if that set up works for you.

Day 35 - A Quiet Space = A Quiet Mind

I hate loud noises. I hate being distracted by people speaking loudly on the phone.

For me, the best environment for maximum productivity is a quiet space.

Here are some spaces I recommend that you try out for yourself:

House

If you work at home, then this is going to be your first choice. For me, I prefer a small space in the corner of the room.

Coffee Shop

I'm personally not a fan of working in coffee shops. I don't thrive in slightly louder places. However, there are a lot of coffee shops nowadays catering mostly for freelancers and work at home professionals.

Co-Working Spaces

Do you feel lonely working alone? Do you want to connect with people in your industry? Then a co-working space is a good place to start. Choose a co-working space where there's ultra-fast wi-fi, slightly quieter than others, and free tea or coffee!

Hotels (Rooms)

If you're working on a special thing, try your luck with hotel rooms. Most hotels tend to not have fast wifi so make sure that what you're about to do doesn't require that you be connected 24/7.

Beach, Cabins & Mountains

This one may cost you a bit more, but sometimes, we just need to have one of those "workation" and have fun while working.

If you're going to do this, start your work with a little walk, then go to work early. Then use the rest of the day to have fun.

Action Guide:

1 - Find the best "quiet space" for you. Try out different locations and then track your progress in each space. Are you getting more things done at a coffee shop? Or do you prefer the serenity of a cabin in the mountain?

2 - Try using an earplug when you're in a coffee shop or a hotel lobby.

Day 36 - Lessen Your Social Media Use

We've already talked about this a little bit but it's so important that we have to discuss this even more. So how do you actually get to quit or at least, lessen your social media? What are the steps that you can implement to achieve your goal of not being distracted by social media every day? What are the things you can do to maximize results?

Action Guide:

1 - Put your phone in another room whenever you're about to do an important task. Put it somewhere where it would require more effort to get your phone back.

2 - Delete your social media apps. Try it for a week at first and see if you can survive without it. Some people can, some people won't.

3 - Schedule your social media time. Instead of trying to fight the urge to use social media, you can schedule your use instead.

Example:
9:00 - 9:30 - Instagram
12-12:30 - Facebook
4:00 -4:30 - Twitter & Instagram

Obviously, the ideal is not to use social media at all. But if you can't do that, you can always start by lessening the amount of time you distract yourself by using social media in the middle of doing a task.

Day 37 - Trick Your Brain to Do Something

One of the hardest things to do is to get started on a project. Whether it's writing every day, working on your business, waking at 4am to practice, etc.

There will always be that force that will pull us down. That force that acts like gravity. We'd rather not write. We'd rather sleep till 10am. We'd rather not do anything at all.

The best trick I know to combat this is to try to do something small. Let's say that you want to run for at least 30 minutes a day. You can start by saying to yourself that you'll only get up. Then once you're already up, your focus is now to grab your running shoes. Then you walk out the door.... And so on...

The goal is to focus on one small step that leads you to do the task you set for yourself.

Make it step by step. Make the process as simple as possible for you. Your goal is not to run for 30 minutes. Your goal starts with standing up and stretching. Then it changes to putting your running shoes, and so on....

Start small and trick your brain to doing what it doesn't want to do.

Action Guide:

1 - Create a breakdown of your own goal. What are the steps that needs to happen for you to actually do them?

Just like in our example above, make it as small a step as possible.

For example, your task is to write a book.

1 - Focus on writing anything.
2 - Then you start by making a paragraph the goal.
3 - Then you move to a page.
4 - Then by the end of your 2-hour writing session, you'll probably have at least 5 pages of materials.

Focus on the small step that will lead you towards achieving your task. That's it, as simple as ABC.

Day 38 - Develop a Sense of Urgency

This one drives me crazy. Why do some people act as if they do not have deadlines? Why do some people act as if they have lots of free time when in reality, they still have a lot of things to do for the day? Why do some people act as if they haven't got enough time to achieve a task but they still manage to waste 4 hours per day on social media?

The root cause of this is a lack of urgency.We think that we have all the time in the world. Well, guess what? We don't.

That's why it's important that we treat our tasks as important. We need to bring back that pride in finishing a task ahead of the deadline. We need to bring back that killer mentality.

It's something that will serve as in the long-term. And we need to develop it every single day.

Action Guide:

1 - Develop a sense of urgency by putting self-imposed deadlines.

2 - Practice by finishing a task ahead of the timeline. This will increase your productivity and give you more extra time for other things that you want to do.

3 - Analyze your officemates. What are they doing with their time? Do they always end up short and always have reasons why they didn't finish the task ahead of the deadline? Look at their response and see if it matches their behavior.

Day 39 - The 20 Second Will Power Method

Okay, this is super simple.

Whenever you don't feel like working on a task at all, just follow the 20-second will power method.

All you have to do is will yourself to work for the next 20 seconds.

Yes, you will force yourself to focus on the task and then work as if someone is going to die if you do not work on your task.

That 20-second bursts of motivation and inspiration can turn into full-blown action. Meaning, once the 20 seconds is done, you are now more likely to work on your task.

You already started it, you already got fired up. Now it's time to continue and finish the task.

Action Guide:

1 - On your next task, once you started to feel that procrastination feeling creeps in, immediately do the 20-second will power method. This will likely fire a motivation inside you and you are now more likely to finish your task. 20 seconds, that's all you need to get that feeling of fire and motivation.

Day 40 - Know the Difference Between Important Vs. Urgent

Just because something is urgent doesn't mean that it's important. In our own professions, we have to know the difference between the two so we'll know what to focus on and what to delegate or not do at all if possible.

IMPORTANT

Important is something that contributes to our mission. Let's say that you're writing a book and your goal is to finish the book within 2 years. You getting interviewed on a TV show may be important, but it's also not urgent. So you'd rather stay at home and write the book instead.

URGENT

Urgent is when you or someone needs to do something quickly. Urgent means there's a deadline coming up and you'll have to pay for the consequences if you don't finish the task on time. Now, the key word here is "consequences." Can you take the negative effect? Is it too big that it will affect your life? If it's not, then it's urgent but not important.

Action Guide:

1 - Identify your tasks whether they are:

A - Important and Urgent

B - Important But Not Urgent

C - Urgent But Not Important

2 - Prioritize doing the tasks that are IMPORTANT & URGENT.

Then the next priority should be Important But Not Urgent. The third one is optional - you can either do it yourself or delegate it to somebody else.

Part 5
Habits to Build for Maximum Productivity

Day 41 - Write Down Your Ideas

Creating a habit of writing down your ideas is something that will serve you, not only in productivity but also in other aspects of your life. I recommend writing ideas because we absolutely cannot remember everything that we think and do.

We need to record our ideas so we'll have a treasure trove of "bullets" to use once we get into the battle. Think of writing down ideas as if you're going into a war. You prepare for it, you study, and you make sure that your ammos are complete.

Having these ideas makes you productive in the sense that you'll spend more time implementing rather than thinking once a problem comes up. These ideas will serve as your ammo for the wars to come.

Action Guide:

1 - Create a habit of listing down ideas at least 2 times a week.

2 - I recommend doing the "top 10 list." A top 10 list is a list of ideas about a certain topic that you can think of.

Example:

Top 10 best movies I ever watched
Top 10 ways to make someone like you
Top 10 ways to make my parents smile
Top 10 ways to double my productivity

Creating a list about different topics prepares your mind to be ready in any problems that you may encounter on work or in every aspect of your life.

Day 42 - Only Check Your Email Once a Day

This is definitely a top 3 productivity killer.

Most emails that we get nowadays are just about other people's agendas. They're asking us to buy this, do this, do that, go here, check this out, etc.

The truth is, 99% of the emails we received are absolute trash. We don't need em'!

Action Guide:

1 - Check your email only at 4pm every day. If not possible, do it at least 2-3 times max! If you're just getting started in trying to lessen your use of email, you can start with this schedule:

Check email for 15 minutes - 11:00-11:15
Check email for 15 minutes - 4:00-4:15
Check email for 15 minutes - 6:30-6:45

2 - Create an autoresponder. If you're super busy, then you need to have some kind of automated response. Personally, I go for short and simple. I say that I'm busy and I don't normally reply to emails anymore. I tell them to send a text or I'll schedule a call with them instead. This makes everything so much faster.

Email is a very limited option when it comes to time and efficiency. If it's that important, then go talk about it face to face or go on a Skype call instead.

3 - Unsubscribe to 90% of your email subscriptions. This alone could save you from 1-2 hours a day of unproductive time.

Day 43 - Conduct Short But Effective Meetings

God, I hate meetings.

9 times out of 10, they're just a waste of time. That's because most meetings are just about random stuff - people joking, people brainstorming ideas, and people without a goal in mind.

Most meetings last from 30-60 minutes when all we really need is 5-10 minutes of focused work.

So how do we fight this phenomenon? How do we not waste our time on nonsense meetings?

Action Guide:

1 - Set a specific goal for the meeting.

Why are we having this meeting? What is the one main thing that we want to achieve? Find out this one thing and all other stuff will be secondary.

2 - Brainstorm ideas even before the meeting. Most meetings are about brainstorming and not about achieving a goal. The key is to disseminate information about the problem even before the meeting starts. By the time a meeting takes place, there should already be ideas ready to solve the main problem.

3 - Set the meeting in advance. There should be at least a 6-hour warning before the meeting. Unexpected meetings tend to be stressful, with too much pressure, and with so little time to

prepare - and it ends up being a circus of people who have nothing to say.

Day 44 - Use Your Calendar

If you're not using your calendar, then you are wasting at least 2-4 hours of productivity time every day. A calendar lets you know about the upcoming tasks. It lets you know the time frame of a certain task, so you'll know exactly when to finish the one that you currently have. The more you follow your calendar, the faster your tasks get done.

For the calendars, I recommend that you put the following in them:

-Meetings with agenda/specific goals
-Tasks/To-Do Lists
-Important Weekly Errands
-Vacations/Leaves

Here's what you don't need to put in them:

-Meetings without agendas
-Unimportant and not urgent tasks

Action Guide:

1 - A desktop app connected to a mobile calendar app is the best way to make sure that your calendar is updated.

Here are two recommended apps that you use:

Google Calendar or Mac & iOS Calendar

Day 45 - Act "As If"

Acting "as if" is a mental exercise that forces your brain to find the best solution to your current problem. Acting as if means you're trying to get closer as much as possible to the best version of yourself.

For example, let's say that you are a consultant.

What are the things that a "productive consultant" often do? What makes a productive consultant? What's the difference between someone who makes $100,000 per year and someone who makes $25,000 as a business consultant?

The key is to act "as if"...

As if you're already a successful consultant.

First, you have to DO before you can BE.

What are the actions that will make you a successful and productive consultant?

List it down and start acting AS IF... as if you're already productive, as if you're already successful, and as if you're already making $100,000 per year.

And then you start doing these action...

This will then lead you to actually becoming a more successful consultant. Instead of faking it till you make it, you're "taking it till ya make it."

The difference is not just in the thinking, but also in the action.

Action Guide:

1 - Practice the idea in your own profession and act "as if."

What does a productive, successful and happy person look like in your own profession? What are the actions he is taking? What is she doing on a daily basis? What are the improvements she's gaining every single week?

Act AS IF you're already that person NOW so one day you'll be better than you already are today.

Day 46 - Walk Outside

Have you ever felt like you just run out of ideas? You can't write anything. You can't seem to move your fingers to actually do your current task...

This only means that you need a break. One of the best use of your break time is by taking a short walk outside your house or office.

The most creative people to ever walk on Earth are the ones who literally has the hobby of walking.

Whether you're a writer, a financial advisor, an ad copywriter, or whatever your job is - walking can help you become more productive and be full of new ideas again.

Action Guide:

1 - Walk outside for 15-20 minutes at least twice a day.

2 - Focus on the scenery and the sound of the environment you are in.

3 - If it's too chaotic, then listen to music with nature as the background music.

4 - Avoid thinking about work. Just be in the moment and walk. Avoid daydreaming about anything and just focus on not getting hit by a bus - sometimes, the best ideas just come out of nowhere.

4 - Immediately write down any ideas that may come up while you are walking.

Day 47 - Stretching Your Body

I always put stretching on my break time. Since I follow the Pomodoro Technique in most of my tasks, I usually have 5-20 minutes of break time. I use at least 2 minutes of my break time to always stretch my whole body.

Stretching de-stresses our body and it helps us in maintaining a healthy posture. You don't want to develop back pain for working 12 hour days just sitting on your office chair. You want to make sure that you move your body every hour and the best way to do that is by having a regular stretching schedule.

Action Guide:

1 - Your stretching schedule doesn't have to be long! Mine is an average of 3-5 minutes per session. Usually, I just do 3 sets of exercises and allot 1 minute per set.

I recommend following the instructions on these links:

https://www.sheknows.com/health-and-wellness/articles/1982060/3-minute-morning-stretching-routine/

https://www.realsimple.com/health/fitness-exercise/stretching-yoga/stretching-exercises

https://www.shape.com/fitness/workouts/only-5-stretches-you-need

Choose the best one for you and don't be afraid to mix them up.

Day 48 - Drink Water Every 1.5 Hours

Drinking water only when you're thirsty is a dangerous game. First of all, if you do that, that means your body is already giving out signals that you're late to the party and it's already drunk. Now it needs its water supply!

You want to regularly replace your body fluid and make sure that you're not dehydrated at any point in time. Dehydration makes your body weak and makes your thinking foggy.

Doctors always recommend 8 glasses of water and I found this to be pretty accurate. Unless you're an athlete of some kind, then you need more than that.

But for mere mortals like us, then 8 glasses is enough.

Action Guide:

1 - I recommend that you drink a glass of water after every 1.5 hours. I found this to be a pretty reasonable and satisfactory in terms of not being dehydrated and not being over hydrated at the same time... either way, find out what works best for you.

2 - Try drinking unsweetened/non-sugar flavored water like the brand **Hint**. Forget about fruit juices, coffee, tea or flavored water with added sugar.

Day 49 - Drink a Green Juice or Smoothie First Thing in the Morning

Green juice or smoothies are all the rage in the past few years. It seems like every hipster in town drinks one.

But don't trash the idea of drinking green juice just yet. The truth is, it's super healthy and everyone should probably be drinking one every day.

What I like about drinking green juice is it gives me extra energy that can last until the end of the day. I found that whenever I don't take my green juice/smoothie, my energy tends to crash by around 1pm. But when I do take my green juice, I get that extra boost that lasts until 7pm. And even then, I feel like I still have the energy to spend time with my family or friends.

In addition, drinking green juice increases my ability to focus. I can concentrate on a task more and I don't feel groggy at any time of the day.

The "power" is just there. It's constant and it's just brewing inside my body like a ball of energy getting stored for later use.

Action Guide:

1 - Find recipes on YouTube and start with the sweeter ones. Once you get acclimated with the taste, start adding more greens and less fruit to your juice or smoothie. The goal is to have a pure green smoothie or juice every single day first thing in the morning. That won't happen overnight. So start with

something sweeter like fruits if you have to. Just make sure that you add more and more green veggies as you get used to drinking juice or smoothie every day.

Day 50 - Pray, Meditate, or Connect

Look, I'm not asking you to be a religious person or anything.

All I want for you is to achieve some kind of peace of mind so you can increase your ability to focus and concentrate on your tasks.

Praying and/or Meditating can help you do that.

Pray

Praying is an act of talking to God. You could be asking for something, for forgiveness, for blessings, for clarity or whatever. If you feel like you are connected to something beyond yourself, then I would consider that as an act of praying.

Meditate

Meditating is about clearing your mind of distraction, worries, stress, and everything that is negative.

I recommend that you start by doing the following routine:

1 - Sit on a quiet corner and put an earplug.

2 - Set a timer on your phone for 3 minutes.

3 - Close your eyes. Breath into your nose and out of your mouth for 3 seconds each for the next 3 minutes.

4 - Focus on the sound and the feeling of your breath.

5 - Increase the amount of time you meditate as you gain more experience and comfortability in meditating.

Action Guide:

1 - Start praying, meditating, connecting or whatever you want to call it. All I ask that you do is you give it a try. Hopefully, something will work for you and you'll continue doing whatever that thing is.

Part 6
Strategies for
Maximum Productivity

Day 51 - Time Blocking

Do you feel like you're spending too much time on a specific task yet you never seem to finish it on time?

You're always hurrying but you're never set for the deadline. You're always hustling but your hustle doesn't seem to get you anywhere closer to your goals.

Well, I have the solution for you. It's called Time Blocking.

Time blocking is simply working by time chunks of 30-50 minutes depending on what you prefer.

The Pomodoro Technique gives you this time frame:

25 Minutes Work
5 Minutes Rest
25 Minutes Work
10 Minutes Rest
25 Minute Work
10 Minutes Rest

Basically, it's about focusing on one task 25 minutes at a time. And then allowing yourself to take a rest for 5-10 minutes after.

This forces your brain to focus on working during the 25 minute time frame.

For the rest time, you should not do anything work-related.

Walk outside, stretch, drink water and do anything non-related to the task you are doing.

Action Guide:

1 - Follow the Pomodoro Technique and start working in time chunks. You'll be amazed at how much you can achieve just by structuring your tasks like this.

2 - Keep testing what works for you. Personally, I found the 25 minute work time to be too short. What I did is I increased it to 50 minutes of work and then 10 minutes of rest. This allows me to focus more and to "keep the ball rolling" since I have more time focused on working.

3 - Rest is important. That 5-15 minutes break that you do throughout the day is considered as important as the work itself. Make sure that you do not skip your breaks unless you're **really in the zone** and you don't want your momentum to change.

Day 52 - Work Chunking

Work Chunking is exactly what it sounds like. It's about structuring a task in a logical sense.

Let's say that you're a copywriter.

Your task for today is to write a short sales page for an eBook you are selling.

Now, a sales page may have different parts like headline, opening, body, offer, closing, price, and guarantee.

Instead of getting overwhelmed by what you have to finish today, you can look at it in chunks and just focus on one chunk at a time.

For the first hour of your day, just focus on headlines. Then on the opening... then on the body... and so on...

The great thing about work chunking is you get to avoid getting overwhelmed. Your goal is not to finish this one gigantic task.

No, your goal is to just focus on one aspect at a time.

This allows your brain to put its effort into just one small task.

Action Guide:

1 - Apply work chunking on your tasks. Especially the ones that require days to finish. Focus on one small task at a time and you'll eventually finish your task at a much more efficient rate.

Day 53 - Batch Your Tasks

Your tasks can be categorized with any of these:

1 - Important and Urgent
2 - Important But Not Urgent
3 - Urgent But Not Important
4 - Extra

The first thing that you should do every day is Important & Urgent tasks. These are the tasks that are going to affect your goals in the short and long term.

The 2nd one are the tasks that's going to affect your results long-term. They may not be urgent now, but if you keep delaying them, eventually, the time will come that it will become Important and Urgent. I recommend that you keep track of your tasks that are on this column.

The third one is urgent but not important. These are tasks that require immediate action. But that action doesn't have to come from you. You can outsource this task to other people. Heck, you may not even have to do this task at all. If it's urgent but not important, then it could be just about other people's agenda.

The last one is the extra. These are the task that is neither important nor urgent. They're just there. You can do them and you can NOT do them if you choose to.

Action Guide:

1 - Categorized your task by any of these 4 and prioritize accordingly. Important and Urgent tasks should always be number one on your to-do list.

Day 54 - Set Your Appointments in Advance

I understand that not all meetings and appointments will be scheduled in advance.

But the more you train people to set an appointment, the fewer distractions you will have.

Appointments are great because you can set the time of the meeting, the place and also the topic of discussion.

As I've told you in the chapter about meetings, nothing kills a meeting than NOT knowing the goals of the meeting.

By scheduling appointments, you can tell them in advance what the goals of the meetings are and you'll waste less time talking about random stuff.

Action Guide:

1 - Always set appointments/meetings in advance. At least 3 days before the meeting is recommended.

2 - Always set a goal for the meeting. What will you guys talk about and what would make the meeting a success? There should always be an end goal in mind. If not, then you're just wasting both of your time.

3 - Use websites like Calendly, Checkfront and Acuity Scheduling to automate your appointments.

Day 55 - Know When to Delegate

Sooner or later, you're going to have to delegate some of your tasks. The more you grow your business, the more you should let other people do some of the work for you.

Look, you might take pride in knowing every single aspect of your business. But the best entrepreneurs know that delegating tasks to people smarter than them is the best way to grow a business.

You can delegate tasks on different aspects of your business like marketing, sales, administrative tasks, and customer service.

Don't be afraid to spend money because the time you will save will give you an advantage when it comes to opportunity cost.

Instead of working hours and hours on your customer's service, you can focus instead on: improving your sales pitch, creating a better product, or even spending more time with your family!

Action Guide:

1 - Look first at freelancing websites like onlinejobs.ph and upwork. You can find pretty much any type of freelancer there. You can get a virtual assistant, appointment setter, sales manager, team manager, etc.

2 - The best freelancers I know are Filipinos. I have many Filipino friends and they are the hardest working and committed people I know.

Day 56 - Sleep Better

We all need 7-8 hours of sleep in order to function at our best. Those people who tell you that you only need 5 hours a day are insane, suicidal and depressed. I know that it's already common advice to sleep 7-8 hours per day, but the question is, is it common practice nowadays?

Probably not. We are in the culture of *hustle till ya make it*. *Work, Work, Work* - that's what we've been taught. But we have to understand that the "rest" part is also an important part of achieving great things.

Action Guide:

1 - Stop using any electronic device 2 hours before you sleep. Doing this alone could make your sleep 2x better!

2 - Make your room as dark as possible. Cover it up as if you're hiding from the world.

3 - Sleep at the same time every night. If you are feeling depressed and always wake up with no energy, you might have an erratic sleeping schedule. If you're only going to implement one advice from this action guide, then this must be it.

4 - If possible, set the room temperature between 60 to 67 Degree Fahrenheit.

5 - Eat your dinner 2-3 hours before you sleep.

6 - Only drink alcohol 4-5 hours before you sleep. Alcohol actually destroys your sleep.

Day 57 - The Slight Edge

Does eating one apple makes you thin? No.

Does eating one slice of pizza make you fat? No.

These are just "small" things that don't really affect you in the short term.

But what if you start eating one slice of pizza every day for the next 365 days? Would that make you fat? Absolutely, yes!

What if you eat one apple a day for the next 2 years? Would that make you healthier? Yes!

The Slight Edge principle works exactly like this. Doing small things over and over again brings in the result - and it could go both ways. Do a bad thing over and over again and it'll give you terrible results within a year. Do that one small thing once and it won't really make a difference.

You can use the slight edge principle to achieve great things and vice versa. The results and the decision to do the right thing is up to you.

Action Guide:

1 - Identify the small things that you can do every day that will have a big impact in the future as long as you continue to do it every single day.

2 - Apply the Slight Edge principle in every aspect of your life. I promise you, you'll be amazed at how much you can achieve in 6-12 months just by following this principle.

Day 58 - Identify Your Bad Habits and Change Them

The most productive people I know aren't perfect. Sometimes, they slide off their path and get distracted by negative stuff.

They start sleeping less, they start eating sugary foods, they stop exercising, they stop time-blocking, etc.

But they also realize and change when these things happen.

They acknowledge that they made a mistake, that they created a bad habit in the process.

After identifying these bad habits, they create a plan to change it. They start applying the principles of *Slight Edge* and start small. Then they go back to their original productive habit.

Action Guide:

1 - Always be aware of what you are doing and not doing. Remember that bad habits are developed over time. The earlier you spot them, the easier changing them will be.

Day 59 - Take a Nap

I call this my secret weapon.

I'm a low energy guy.

I always start the day with "enough" energy to last till 12nn especially when I don't drink my morning juice or smoothie.

To combat this, I always take a nap at around 12:40-1pm. Doing this allows me to continue my work with full of energy. When I nap, I can usually still be effective at my work until 6pm.

How much more can you achieve knowing that you'll still be efficient and effective after lunch? Most people are already dead tired at this point - and napping solves that problem

Action Guide:

1 - Take a nap during lunch. Nap no more than 20 minutes or this will have a negative effect on you instead.

2 - Set a timer so you don't sleep past 20 minutes. If you go past 20 minutes, then you'll probably end up groggy and irate.

Day 60 - Set a Not-To-Do List

As important as to do lists are, you also have to have an idea of things you should stop doing.

These are the things that cause you to be less productive. These are the things that makes you procrastinate.

For example, part of my NOT TO DO LISTS are:

1 - Watching Netflix every day
2 - Browsing social media more than 1 hour a day
3 - checking my email more than 2 times per day
4 - Eating junk food

This list serves as a reminder to keep doing the stuff that only helps me achieve my goal. Obviously, I'm not perfect at this. But just by simply creating this list, I now know exactly what things I may encounter that will NOT serve my purpose.

Action Guide:

1 - Create a NOT TO DO list every week. You don't need to create a NOT TO DO list every day since it might likely just cost you time. However, a weekly not to do list will serve as a reminder of things not to do - so you'll have more time doing what's best for you.

Conclusion

Building *Maximum Productivity* isn't some kind of "ALL IN OR NOT" situation.

The best thing about improving your productivity is you can do it by bits and pieces.

On the first week, you can apply 3 ideas from this book. Then you do 2 more on the 2nd week... and so on...

Another thing is you don't necessarily have to apply them all!

Just 5-10 ideas from this book can easily double your productivity and your results.

So don't get overwhelmed by all the information in this book.

Choose 1 or 2 to try and see if it'll work for you.

That's all I ask you to do. Try some ideas and see the results for yourself. If I'm a betting man, I'll say that applying 5 ideas from this book will give you at least 2 hours per day of "free time" that you can use on something else besides work. What you use in that "free time" is up to you.

All the best,

A.V. Mendez

OTHER BOOKS

Author's page:

https://www.amazon.com/A.V.-Mendez/e/B00XU2UW5S/